DORI SANDERS' COUNTRY COOKING

Also by Dori Sanders

Clover
Her Own Place

DORI SANDERS' COUNTRY COOKING
RECIPES AND STORIES FROM THE FAMILY FARM STAND

BY DORI SANDERS

consulting editor, John Willoughby

Algonquin Books of Chapel Hill   2003

Published by
ALGONQUIN BOOKS OF CHAPEL HILL
Post Office Box 2225
Chapel Hill, North Carolina 27515-2225

a division of
WORKMAN PUBLISHING
708 Broadway
New York, New York 10003

LIBRARY OF CONGRESS CATALOGING-IN-PUBLICATION DATA
Sanders, Dori, 1934–
Dori Sanders' country cooking : recipes and stories from the family
farm stand / by Dori Sanders.
p.   cm.
Includes index.
ISBN 1-56512-117-1 (hardcover)
1. Cookery, American—Southern style.   2. Farm life—South Carolina.
3. Country life—South Carolina.   I. Title.
TX715.2.S68S26   1995
641.5975—dc20   95–32796
                                                            CIP
ISBN 1-56512-385-9

10 9 8 7 6 5 4 3 2 1
First Paperback Edition

To my sister Virginia,
who has picked, prepared, and tested
right alongside me from the first page to the very last,

and with enormous gratitude to John Willoughby,
without whom this book would never have been completed . . .

and that's the whole truth!

CONTENTS

INTRODUCTION

I still live on the farm where I was born—a farm that has been in our family for more than seventy years. Here in York County, South Carolina, our family spends many hours working together—planting and harvesting and running the farm stand where we sell peaches, okra, crowder peas, and all the other wonderful produce we grow. Often when we're working we find ourselves talking about the past, and what we seem to remember most is the food.

Whenever we talk about food—or whenever we eat, for that matter—we always think of our Great-Aunt Vestula. Over the years we have shared so many memories of her, and they still surface every time we gather together.

Aunt Vestula worked in the Low Country of South Carolina, down near Charleston, in the earlier part of this century. We don't know exactly where or for whom, but we do know that she worked in the kitchen of a very, very wealthy plantation owner.

On her visits to our home in Up-Country, Aunt Vestula brought with her the most wonderful and exciting foods we could ever have dreamed of, recipes that used things in ways we'd never imagined. Adding just a touch of sherry to this dish, a drop of wine to that, using fresh herbs and capers, grating a smidgen of nutmeg into a soup or a stew, my Aunt Vestula changed the way we thought about cooking.

Recently one of my sisters and I toured South Carolina's Low Country. As we viewed the old plantation mansions, we couldn't help wondering, was it here? was it there? that our Aunt Vestula was introduced to the wonderful things she cooked. What family was it that influenced her cooking methods and the knowledge she passed on to our family?

Even as my sister and I traveled on over into Georgia and then back up through South Carolina to our home near the North Carolina border, we kept looking across the long acres of land near every mansion and wondered whether Aunt Vestula had lived in some small house there. We searched for clues but returned home empty-handed.

We still have our memories of her, though. I will never forget the last time Aunt Vestula traveled up from the Low Country to our home. That time it was not for a visit; our Aunt Vestula came to stay. The memory is fresh and vivid in my mind, at once sad and happy. And so I remember, and nearly always, I laugh.

On that last visit, the only things Aunt Vestula brought with her were the most beautiful trunk I had ever seen and the memory of the plantation mistress for whom she had worked. She remembered how the mistress had managed the household, the way she would direct the servants in the morning, the way she ordered her day, the way she expected the meals to be prepared and the table spread.

By the time Aunt Vestula moved in with us, she was too feeble to cook, but she was always in the kitchen when my mama was cooking. During the cold days of the one winter she lived with us, she would sit tall and regal on a cane-bottomed, straight-backed chair in a warm corner near the wood-burning cookstove, her head held high. In the spring and summer she maintained her presence in the kitchen, but her chair was moved to an open window.

Aunt Vestula had many dresses, but it was hard to tell because they all looked so much alike: muted plaids with lots of blue, or plain blue with tiny little flowers. In the winter the dresses were of soft cotton flannel; in the summer they were made of lawn, that soft, airy, old-fashioned fabric, perfect for hot weather.

While my mama cooked, Aunt Vestula tried to instruct her. A most obliging, patient student was my mama. Aunt Vestula often reminded her to pick a few shallots or leeks to saute along with the fresh wild mushrooms, or to be sure to add just a little mild sherry. Aunt Vestula would go on and on, not noticing that my mama usually didn't follow through on anything she said.

But sometimes my mama *would* cut up an onion or a clove of garlic that she hadn't planned on using. She never added wine because she hardly ever had any, but she would grate a smidgen of nutmeg over meat and vegetables. Aunt Vestula was so accustomed to that taste that my mama was afraid Aunt Vestula would notice if it wasn't added and complain.

During the hot summer afternoons, Aunt Vestula would sometimes sit on the front porch in her wicker rocking chair and gaze across the open fields. From time to time she would call out to my mama that she was late bringing her afternoon tea and biscuits. I don't remember all that went on in the kitchen, but I surely do remember those afternoons on the front porch, when I would wait for Aunt Vestula to give me a bite of her tea cake.

Sometimes Aunt Vestula would worry that the field-workers were thirsty—surely they would enjoy a nice cup of tea. But then she would remind herself that there were too many of them, far too many, to serve tea to. My mama said Aunt Vestula sometimes truly believed that she was the mistress of a large plantation and that my mama was the cook, as Aunt Vestula herself had once been.

I don't have to second-guess where my mama got her ideas for the Sunday afternoon silver teas, the box suppers, and the other fancy events of our rural life. I know. My mama once said she so wished she had asked Aunt Vestula all her questions about cooking when she had a chance. I remember Mama voicing her regrets: "If only I'd asked her how to make this," "If only I'd asked her how to make that." I remember her wishing she could capture the exact taste of Aunt Vestula's roasted peppers, the liver pudding, the feather-light pumpkin mousse, the scone-like lemon biscuits.

I now understand my mama's regret. Although I pull up what sage wisdom I can from the past, it seems to have few roots, and I wish there were a way I could ask Aunt Vestula some questions of my own. As someone once wrote, "So rare had been the chance to learn. So rare the chance to learn." And so soon the opportunity had passed.

But I can still turn to the farming life for roots, for those influences and traditions that have remained basically the same through the years. Today we farmers still subsist mostly off the fruit of the land, living from harvest to harvest just as in earlier times. And unlike what so many people think, we Southern farmers don't—and never did—eat our food swimming in sugar and fat. Oh, we did use butter and sugar and bacon when I was a child, but only for special events. Most days we had to come up with recipes that didn't call for much fat or sugar. We ate lots of fresh fruits and vegetables and had many a meatless meal. Cooking ingredients had to be stretched in a large family like ours. But there were always Sundays and company just ahead, and those were the times for really, really good, rich cooking.

In my recipes, it's easy to find the influence of my childhood. I grew up the eighth of ten children, with five brothers and four sisters. With that many children in the household and only two milk cows, every bit of sweet milk was churned to get butter for the family table. For cooking and drinking we used the buttermilk left after churning. So I have lots of recipes that use buttermilk, which makes the dishes lighter. Many of my recipes also include lots of fresh herbs and little sugar. Like my mother before me, though, I do cook rich foods when company is coming, so you will find both types of recipes here.

Like most farm-family cooks, I don't measure or fuss too much with details. How much of an ingredient? Enough for one good mess, a couple of handfuls or so. What size pan? Whatever I have handy. If it's too small, I just cut down on the amount I'm going to cook. If it's too big, I end up with something cooked for tomorrow as well.

But please know that for this book I have measured and checked to be sure that the recipes here make the foods that I have in mind. If you're a family cook like I am, though, feel free to change "½ cup" to "one handful" in your mind, and make these recipes the way you'll like them best.

My approach to cooking is simple because for the most part our foods are simple. But that doesn't mean our foods are boring. Oh, no, they're not. To the gourmet chef who cooks with wine, fresh vegetables, and herbs grown in her own garden, I say, well, we cook that way, too. Been doing it for years. But I must confess, even though a number of my recipes include wine (especially the ones from Aunt Vestula), our family's bottles rarely make it to the stove. Whether our wine is home-made or store-bought, we usually decide it can be used in a better way than for cooking.

As a hard-working farmer, let me tell you, the farming life leaves precious few hours for anything but simple cooking. So I am pretty much stuck in the past. I still cook the basic, simple survival foods, dishes that brought us through the Great Depression and the hard times of failed crops and lean harvests.

Our original family home no longer stands. The old wood-burning cookstove has rusted into pieces. The silver teas are a thing of the past. But precious recipes are still intact, and the tastes and smells of the foods of my childhood let me know that I can go back again. I hope that this collection of recipes and memories will take you back, too, to a world of old-fash-ioned family cooking and Southern country warmth and hospitality.

CHAPTER 1

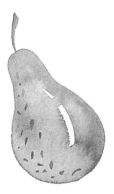

Visits from Aunt Vestula

I can't remember how Aunt Vestula traveled to our home when she came up from the South Carolina Low Country. I now know that she must have come by train, but back then we children never saw her until she walked into our front yard. Everything had to be "just so" for her visit, which meant we were all kept busy putting things in order the day of her arrival while Father went to the train station. Besides, if all ten children had gone to pick her up, there would have been no place for her to sit on the way home. So my father would go alone to get her in whatever vehicle he had at the time, and suddenly, there she'd be!

As soon as she arrived she would start unpacking the gifts she had brought. I always got a little tea set. If I hadn't broken every single piece in every single set, I would now have quite a collection. To this day I rarely drink a cup of tea without thinking of my Aunt Vestula.

Aunt Vestula's visits always brought great joy, and for good reason. She arrived well stocked not only with gifts but also with wonderful foods. You see, my Aunt Vestula cooked for the rich—the very rich.

I especially remember the seafood she would bring, carefully packed in giant wicker hampers that opened like suitcases and had handles on the side. My cousin Will Mack claims that the seafood was packed in smoking dry ice to survive the long journey. There would be mackerel and shrimp and other fish fresh from the Atlantic Ocean. Often there would be freshly shucked oysters, too. Some of the oysters were for stewing, while others were for frying, but there were always enough to make skillet oyster dressing as well.

The seafood Aunt Vestula brought with her was expensive and ever so special, so you know it was for grown-ups only. But my siblings and I didn't mind, because Aunt Vestula always made us her special "seafood" fried chicken, which marinated overnight in a mixture of buttermilk and seafood seasoning. "Still tastes just like fish," she always reminded us as she dished up the fried chicken. And it did.

Of course, in Aunt Vestula's wicker hamper there was always a great big fruitcake wrapped in heavy, brandy-soaked brown paper and stored in a decorative airtight tin. Sometimes Aunt Vestula even brought little lemon-filled cookies baked in cups made from brown paper bags. We would eat the little pielike cookies and then lick every crumb from those brown-paper-bag cups.

Our mother later made those same cookies. She'd save every little brown paper bag that survived a trip from the store still clean enough to be used for baking. Usually the ones that survived had carried only a few tacks or some dried seeds. Mama would cut the tops off the bags and use them to line muffin tins for those delicious lemon cookies.

When I remember all the food that Aunt Vestula brought and the way she so carefully packed it, I think that the plantation owners for whom she worked must have been some kind of good to her. You see, it was only through their generosity that she could have brought us all those wonderful foods.

But you must also know that Aunt Vestula worked at a time when the "pay and tote" system was in effect. It was just a little Southern thing. "Pay" was the amount of money you received for your services, "tote" was the extra food you carried home to your own family. Cooks during that time always prepared a little bit more food than necessary for the family they worked for. That way they were guaranteed to have some food to tote home. They simply added a little more sugar to the pound than necessary. It wasn't considered stealing; it was understood as part of their wages.

After Aunt Vestula passed out presents to the children, my mama would join her in the kitchen to unpack those hampers full of food. It didn't seem to bother our mama in the least that Aunt Vestula took over when she visited. When Aunt Vestula was in residence, the kitchen belonged to her. My mama was her helper. Aunt Vestula would cook, give orders, and nearly always complain that my mama's eggbeater was of no account and that even peach switches could beat egg whites better.

So the women cooked. And cooked. Sliding pots and pans across the smooth surface of the wood-burning stove, laughing and remembering, they'd talk about the food they'd cooked for quilting bees and corn shuckings and hog killings. They'd recall the most recent box supper and plan for the next silver tea. For these two women, food—and the joy it brought when shared with family and friends—was truly the center of their lives. For many farm women, it still is. Some things time does not change.

THE RECIPES

Cool Cucumber Soup

"Smells Like Sunday" Chicken
Fricassee with Meatballs

Aunt Vestula's Little Noodles

Sauteed Shad Roe with
Onions and Garlic

Aunt Vestula's "Chicken into
Seafood" Seasoning Blend

Batter-Fried Frog Legs

Baked Cucumber Slices

Turnip Slaw

Skillet Crackling Bread

Watermelon and Cantaloupe
with Brandy

Pecan Pie with Black
Walnut Crust

COOL CUCUMBER SOUP
Serves 4

I'm so entrenched in the past, I often hesitate to pull my sister's food processor down from the pantry shelf, and instead hand-mix many recipe ingredients. For some reason, they just seem to taste better that way. For this delicious, cooling summer soup, there is no better "processor" than a half-gallon Ball Mason jar, which you can use as a mixer just like Aunt Vestula did.

2 cucumbers, roughly chopped
4 cups buttermilk
1 tablespoon finely chopped fresh dill
1 tablespoon finely chopped fresh parsley
⅛ teaspoon ground white pepper, or to taste

Place all the ingredients in a clean, sterilized ½-gallon glass jar. Screw the lid on firmly and shake vigorously to blend. Refrigerate until well chilled, at least 1 hour. Shake the jar again just before serving.

"SMELLS LIKE SUNDAY" CHICKEN FRICASSEE WITH MEATBALLS

Serves 4

Like many of our family recipes, this one was created out of the need to stretch ingredients. One day when there was just a little chicken and even less ground beef in the house, Aunt Vestula decreed that the two should be cooked together to make a meal large enough for the family. The resulting wonderfully tasty dish smelled just like Sunday dinner, but it wasn't, because on Sundays we always made sure to have enough of either chicken or meat. But it is still one of my absolute favorite ways to cook chicken.

1 ½ pounds boneless chicken thighs, skin removed
¾ cup plus 2 teaspoons all-purpose flour
⅛ teaspoon salt
⅛ teaspoon freshly ground black pepper
¼ teaspoon dried oregano
¼ teaspoon dried thyme
½ teaspoon garlic powder (optional)
4 tablespoons vegetable oil
1 cup chopped onion
8 to 10 meatballs (page 7)
½ cup chicken stock
⅓ cup dry white wine

1. Wash the chicken and pat it dry. In a shallow baking pan, combine ¾ cup flour and the salt, pepper, oregano, thyme, and, if desired, garlic powder and mix well. Dredge the chicken thighs in this mixture to coat, shaking off any excess seasoned flour.

2. In a large skillet, heat the oil over medium-high heat until hot but not smoking. Add the chicken and brown on both sides, about 4 minutes per side. Remove and set aside.

3. Pour off the oil from the skillet, leaving only a thin layer. Add the chopped onion and saute over medium-high heat, stirring occasionally, until tender and lightly browned, about 8 minutes. Stir in the 2 teaspoons of flour and blend well.

4. Return the chicken to the skillet, add the meatballs, stock, and wine, and stir gently to blend. Cover and braise over moderate heat, stirring occasionally, for 45 minutes or until the chicken and meatballs are cooked through. Adjust seasoning and serve with rice or little noodles (page 9).

MEATBALLS
Makes 8 to 10

½ cup bread crumbs
3 tablespoons milk
½ pound lean ground beef
Salt and freshly ground black pepper to taste
1 small onion, chopped
⅛ teaspoon poultry seasoning (optional)
2 tablespoons vegetable oil

1. In a large bowl, combine the bread crumbs and milk and mix well. Add the beef, salt, pepper, onion, and poultry seasoning and mix until well combined. Form the mixture into balls about 1 ½ inches in diameter.

2. In a large skillet, heat the oil over medium-high heat until hot but not smoking. Add the meatballs in a single layer and cook, turning occasionally, until well browned on all sides, about 7 to 8 minutes. Remove from the skillet, drain on paper towels, and add to the chicken fricassee as directed in step 4, previous page.

Christmas Decorations

Aunt Vestula decorated our house for the holidays with the same ritualistic fervor as when she cooked. She would get my daddy to cut a perfect, cone-shaped cedar tree and bring it into the living room. First she placed a wisp of field cotton near the base of each branch. Nobody else in Filbert, South Carolina, put their cotton on the tree that way. Everybody else put it on the outer tips of the branches, but Aunt Vestula tucked it all the way down by the trunk. Next she went out-doors and gathered small branches from other cedar trees, choosing those with the most dusty, silvery-blue cedar berries. She would tie these little branches onto the tree, along with pinecones and some sprigs of holly with glossy, spiky leaves and bright red berries. Then she would take short lengths of old, used lace—never longer than a yard—and drape them over a few branches. She would cover the ends of the lace with big bows made of white crepe paper, shred-ding the streamers that trailed from the bows with a fork to make ribbons. For the finishing touch, Aunt Vestula polished dried honey locust pods to a beautiful mahogany color, threaded them onto a string and festooned the branches with them. My sister Virginia follows this tradition to this day.

Aunt Vestula placed additional sprays of cedar branches, pine-cones, and holly with berries all over the house—on and above the mantle, in every window, and even in small wooden kegs. Finally, Aunt Vestula tied streamers cut from crisply starched gingham and calico cloth around the stair rail-ings, with bows attached here and there from top to bottom, a custom she brought from South Carolina's Low Country where she worked. Only then was the house ready for the holidays.

AUNT VESTULA'S LITTLE NOODLES
Serves 4

Our Aunt Vestula used to make these tiny butter-fried noodles to serve under her chicken fricassee with meatballs. You can try them with any kind of stew dish, though.

2 large eggs
¾ cup water
⅛ teaspoon freshly grated nutmeg
Salt and freshly ground black pepper to taste
1 ½ cups all-purpose flour
2 tablespoons unsalted butter

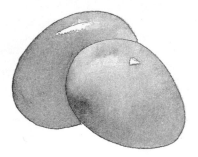

1. In a medium bowl, combine the eggs, water, nutmeg, salt, and pepper. Using a wire whisk, mix together until well blended. Add the flour in three parts, whisking until smooth after each addition.

2. In a medium saucepan, bring about 1 ½ quarts of water to a boil over high heat. Add salt to taste. Pour the noodle batter into a colander, hold the colander over the boiling water, and press the batter through the holes of the colander with a wooden spoon until all the batter has been pressed through.

3. Cook until the noodles rise to the surface, about 5 to 6 minutes. Using a slotted spoon, remove the noodles to a large bowl filled with ice water to stop them from cooking further. As soon as the noodles are cool, drain them well.

4. In a skillet, melt the butter over medium heat. Add the noodles and cook, stirring constantly, until lightly browned, about 4 minutes. Serve immediately.

SAUTEED SHAD ROE WITH ONIONS AND GARLIC
Serves 4

When Aunt Vestula visited in the spring, my parents were sure to buy some shad roe, although as children we weren't allowed to eat any because it was so expensive.

Shad roe usually comes in pairs of roe sacs that hold the tiny, delicate eggs. When preparing the sacs, be very careful not to break the membrane and release the eggs.

3 pairs shad roe
¼ cup milk
Salt and freshly ground black pepper to taste
2 tablespoons white cornmeal
2 tablespoons all-purpose flour
3 tablespoons vegetable oil
1 large onion, halved, then thinly sliced
1 tablespoon finely chopped garlic
1 tablespoon fresh lemon juice

1. In a shallow baking dish, combine the milk, salt, and pepper and mix well. In a second shallow baking dish, combine the cornmeal and flour and mix well. Dip the roe first into the milk mixture, then into the cornmeal mixture, coating all sides.

2. In a heavy skillet, heat 2 tablespoons of the oil over medium-high heat until hot but not smoking. Add the roe and cook on one side until golden-brown, about 2 to 3 minutes. Carefully turn the roe and cook for 2 to 3 minutes more. Cover the pan and continue to cook until the roe is cooked through and shows clear, about 3 to 4 minutes. Transfer to a warm plate.

3. In the same skillet, heat the remaining oil until hot but not smoking. Add the onions and cook, stirring occasionally, until tender and lightly browned, about 8 minutes. Add the garlic and cook, stirring frequently, for an additional minute. Add the lemon juice, stir to blend well, and spoon the mixture over the roe. Serve immediately.

AUNT VESTULA'S "CHICKEN INTO SEAFOOD" SEASONING BLEND

Makes about ½ cup

Somehow this particular combination of herbs and spices always made chicken taste just like seafood to us children. Even if it doesn't have the same effect for you, it will surely make your chicken delicious.

2 tablespoons finely crushed bay leaves
5 tablespoons celery salt
1 tablespoon dry mustard
1 tablespoon freshly ground black pepper
1 ½ teaspoons ground nutmeg
1 teaspoon ground cloves
1 teaspoon ground ginger
1 tablespoon paprika
1 teaspoon ground red pepper
½ teaspoon ground mace

Combine all the ingredients, mix well, and store in an airtight half-pint Ball Mason jar. If stored in a cool, dark place, the seasoning blend will keep for at least 1 month. To use, marinate chicken in buttermilk overnight, then rub well with the seasoning blend and fry using your usual method or the recipe for Buttermilk Southern Fried Chicken on page 135.

BATTER-FRIED FROG LEGS
Serves 4

Yes, this recipe does serve four, because frog legs are really rich. When I was a child, my daddy and brothers would catch frogs in the streams and creeks around our farm. With our large family, though, they seldom caught enough for everyone, so we pulled straws for the chance to share the legs.

8 frog legs
1 teaspoon active dry yeast
1 cup lukewarm water
1 cup all-purpose flour
½ teaspoon salt, or to taste
½ teaspoon ground white pepper, or to taste
½ cup shortening or vegetable oil for frying

1. In a small bowl, dissolve the yeast in the lukewarm water and allow to stand for 3 or 4 minutes. Add the flour, salt, and pepper and beat until thoroughly mixed. Let the batter stand at room temperature for about 1 ½ hours.

2. Wash the frog legs well in cold water, then use a sharp knife to peel the skin from the legs. (It should strip off easily, like a glove.) Place the skinned legs in a medium saucepan, pour enough boiling water into the pan to cover the legs, then drain at once and pat dry with paper towels.

3. In a large, heavy skillet, heat the shortening or oil over medium-high heat until hot but not smoking. Dip the frog legs in the batter, turning to coat well, and fry until golden-brown and cooked through, about 4 to 6 minutes. Drain on paper towels and serve immediately.

BAKED CUCUMBER SLICES
Serves 4

We didn't have a refrigerator in our house when I was young. In fact, I was grown before we even got electricity. So raw salads with mayonnaise or other dressings were not common. Instead, uncooked vegetables were usually marinated in vinegar. We tended to cook most vegetables, though, including cucumbers. You can use this recipe for squash, too. If you do, it would greatly please one of my brothers, who loves what he calls "squashy casserole."

4 medium cucumbers
Salt and freshly ground black pepper to taste
2 tablespoons olive oil
1 cup croutons, finely crushed, or 1 cup herbed bread crumbs
3 green onions (including green part), finely chopped

1. Preheat oven to 450° F.

2. Cut both ends off the cucumbers. Stand them on end and, with a sharp knife, cut a thin slice from each side to remove the skin and make the cucumber "square." Cut the cucumbers lengthwise into slices about ¼ inch thick. Sprinkle with salt and pepper and set aside.

3. Place the olive oil in a large, shallow baking pan. Dip the cucumber slices into the oil to cover lightly, then dip into the crushed croutons or bread crumbs to coat evenly, shaking off any excess crumbs.

4. Pour the oil out of the baking pan, leaving a thin coating, and lay the cucumber slices in the pan. Bake until tender and golden-brown, about 8 to 10 minutes. Turn with a spatula and cook until the other side is also browned, about 5 to 7 minutes more.

5. Remove the cucumber slices from the oven, drain well on paper towels, sprinkle with the chopped green onions, and serve hot.

TURNIP SLAW
Serves 4 to 6

With turnips, as with many other vegetables, it's either feast or famine, and you struggle to serve them in different ways when they are abundant. I find this recipe a delightful change from standard salads, and it works so well during the winter months when you definitely need a little salad.

3 or 4 medium turnips
2 stalks celery
2 green onions, with bottoms trimmed but green parts left on
½ cup buttermilk
2 tablespoons vegetable oil
1 tablespoon fresh lemon juice
⅛ teaspoon salt, or to taste
⅛ teaspoon freshly ground black pepper, or to taste
2 tablespoons capers, drained
1 teaspoon chopped fresh sage
1 tablespoon chopped fresh parsley

1. Peel the turnips and cut first into quarters, then into very thin strips. Place in a medium saucepan, add enough water to cover, and bring to a boil over medium-high heat. Blanch until just tender, 2 to 3 minutes, drain, and set aside in a large bowl.

2. Slice the celery and green onions at a sharp angle and as thinly as possible. Add to the bowl of turnips.

3. In a medium bowl, combine the buttermilk, oil, lemon juice, salt, and pepper. Mix until smooth. Add the capers, sage, and parsley and stir gently. Pour this dressing over the turnip mixture, toss gently, and serve.

The Christmas Give

Aunt Vestula and my grandparents provided us with many traditions. One of my favorites was the "Christmas give." By this tradition, you knocked on your friends' doors during the Christmas season, and as soon as the door opened a crack, you yelled, "Christmas give!"

Sometimes children would yell it out as soon as they heard someone coming to answer the door, but by the rules you were supposed to wait until the door began to open. Anyway, nine times out of ten you could beat the person who opened the door—they wanted you to be first so they could invite you in.

Then they had to offer you the "Christmas give." For the visiting grown-ups this meant thick slices of cake and sassafras tea or wild persimmon beer; for the children it was usually a little handful from a basket of fruits and nuts and candy kept near the door throughout the Christmas season. This little farm-country tradition always made Christmas more fun.

SKILLET CRACKLING BREAD

Serves 4 to 6, but in some households only 1

In Southern families, crackling (don't say the "g") bread is a favorite. You must have at least a cake or two of it during the winter season. For those who don't know, cracklings are chewy nuggets of baconlike fresh hog meat. Many stores sell cracklings these days, but you can also make your own by cooking half a pound of salt pork or thick slab bacon in a heavy cast-iron skillet over medium heat until it has rendered all its fat, about ten minutes. The crisp, browned bits that remain after draining the fat are the cracklings. In this recipe for crackling bread, you can substitute chicken cracklings, which you can make by following the directions in "Stretching the Meat" (page 58).

Crackling bread is great when served with turnip or mustard greens, because you want something with a little bite to go with the rich bread.

1 ½ cups white or yellow cornmeal
1 ¼ cups milk
1 egg
3 teaspoons baking powder
2 tablespoons all-purpose flour
¾ cup cracklings

1. Preheat oven to 450° F.

2. In a large bowl, combine all the ingredients and beat thoroughly. Pour into a large, well-greased cast-iron skillet and bake in the preheated oven for about 25 minutes or until golden-brown. Remove from oven and serve hot.

WATERMELON AND CANTALOUPE WITH BRANDY
Serves 6

I must confess, it was only recently that I tried this recipe. I grew up thinking that if you mixed watermelon with any form of alcohol it would be a deadly combination. A lot of people in our area still think this. This recipe is not from my Aunt Vestula or from my mother. I concocted it because I remembered that Aunt Vestula once sprinkled a little brandy over pieces of watermelon in a bowl, ate the watermelon, and *lived*.

4 cups watermelon cubes, seeds removed
⅓ cup brandy
¼ cup cassis or sloe gin
3 small cantaloupes, chilled
6 sprigs fresh mint for garnish (optional)

1. Place the watermelon cubes in a large bowl, sprinkle with the brandy and cassis or sloe gin, and toss gently. Cover and refrigerate overnight.

2. Cut the cantaloupes in half, scoop out the seeds, and remove the flesh with a melon baller. Mix the melon balls with the watermelon.

3. Mound the watermelon and cantaloupe in the cantaloupe shells and serve garnished with mint sprigs, if desired.

PECAN PIE WITH BLACK WALNUT CRUST

Serves 6 to 8

When our locally grown black walnuts are harvested, I hull them and spread them outside on cardboard to dry in the sun. The hulling leaves my fingernails stained for about a week, but this recipe is so wonderful, it's worth it. It's particularly tasty when topped with honey-ginger whipped cream.

3 eggs
½ cup packed light or dark brown sugar
1 teaspoon vanilla extract
½ cup all-purpose flour
1 cup dark corn syrup (you can substitute light)
½ cup light corn syrup
2 cups pecans, broken into pieces,
plus additional whole pecans for garnish, if desired
1 black walnut pie crust (page 21)

For the whipped cream topping:

8 ounces heavy cream
1 teaspoon ground ginger
2 teaspoons honey

1. Preheat oven to 350° F.
2. In a medium bowl, combine the eggs, brown sugar, and vanilla and

mix well. Add the flour and mix well. Add the dark and light corn syrups and the pecan pieces and mix until well blended.

3. Pour the filling into the prepared pie crust and, if desired, top with whole pecans. Bake in the preheated oven for 20 to 25 minutes or until the pie filling is set.

4. Meanwhile, in a chilled medium bowl, whip the cream, ginger, and honey together until the cream forms stiff peaks, about 5 minutes if using an electric mixer set on high.

5. Remove pie from oven and cool on a wire rack. When cool, remove tart pan sides. Serve with the honey-ginger whipped cream.

BLACK WALNUT PIE CRUST
Makes one 10-inch pie shell

1 ½ cups crushed black walnuts
1 cup unsalted butter, softened
5 tablespoons sugar
2 cups all-purpose flour
2 egg yolks, beaten
1 teaspoon vanilla extract
About 1 teaspoon water

1. In a medium bowl, combine all the ingredients and mix well. The mixture should resemble cookie dough. If it does not, add a bit more flour or water as needed.

2. Turn the dough out into a well-greased 10-inch tart pan with a removable bottom. Using your hands, press the dough from the center out toward the sides of the pan, making sure to cover the bottom and sides of the pan as evenly as possible.

3. Cover and refrigerate for at least 1 hour before using. Do not freeze this pie crust.

Snow Cream

When I was young, before the local weather patterns changed, we had really cold winters in Filbert, South Carolina. Yes, we even had snow. We always looked forward to it, especially because we made homemade snow ice cream. We called it "snow cream."

These days, I find myself wishing for the now-rare snowstorm. At the first sight of a snowflake in the sky, I immediately make plans for a dessert party. I invite nearby family members, coax one of them to make warm honey gingerbread and another to build a big fire in the fireplace, and I watch the skies, hoping for lots of snow. While I wait for the snow to accumulate, I make a boiled custard and set it in the refrigerator to chill.

And if enough snow does fall, I dress warmly, pull on heavy boots, and head far from the traveled roads to the hills on our family farm. There I gather a big pail of clean, fresh-fallen snow and rush home to stir it into the custard along with extra chilled milk to make snow cream. Smooth, rich, thick, and creamy, it is a wonderful reminder of childhood.

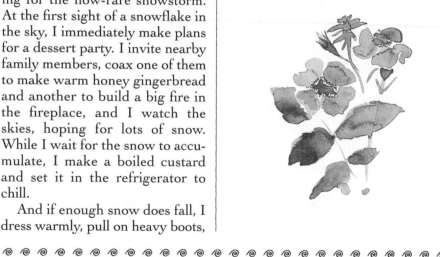

CHAPTER 2

A Corn-Shucking Supper

As hard as life can be on a farm, it is also wonderfully rewarding in so many little ways. I love when the fields are being readied for planting, when the first shoots of sweet potato plants appear, when the peaches are ripe and ready to be picked. I also love meeting people at our farm stand, and I especially enjoy when they come to buy corn.

The only kind of corn the young people know about is sweet corn, but many of our older customers still ask for field corn. We call it "mule corn" or "roasting ears," because in the old days we planted it for the table and for the mules. Until there were hybrids, this was the only kind of corn we had. We still raise it, and I daresay that if our mules had to depend on it they would go hungry, because we generally sell every ear that we harvest.

One variety of mule corn that we raise is "trucker's favorite," which got its name because the truckers love how it holds up so well. It has a very thick husk, so you can knock it around a bit, and when you finally take the husk off, the tiny white kernels inside will still be oh, so tender. Another variety is called "limber cob." It's wonderful for making corncob jelly because the cobs are so long, soft, and limber that you can bend them around until they almost make a circle and they still won't break.

Northerners generally hate mule corn, but we have plenty of Southern farmers who come in and request it by the bagful. They like it so much that we can't keep it at the stand. And talk about pure corn flavor! You haven't really tasted corn until you've tried mule corn. It makes the very best homemade creamed corn and fried corn and summer corn chutney.

With any kind of corn, you must be sure to pick it at its peak moment of ripeness. If it is allowed to get overripe, the kernels will pucker the day after it is pulled. We farmers keep careful watch over the fields. Some of my neighbors still use the "raccoon test" to determine when their corn is ready to pull. Raccoons will not eat corn before its time, but the minute it's ready they go right after it. So, as soon as the raccoons venture into the fields, the farmer gets out there and picks the corn as fast as possible.

These days the full summer work schedule on the farm often robs me of the time to prepare many of the corn-based foods I so love. But each fall, under the harvest moon, local farmers still gather at one another's corn-filled cribs for "corn shuckings," gatherings where fun, food, and drink make work seem like play. And corn shuckings offer a chance for farm wives to show off their cooking and baking skills. You see, on a farm, cooking is usually our greatest outlet.

My paternal grandmother, who was of Native American heritage, used corn in *all* the foods she cooked for corn-shucking suppers. My paternal grandfather used corn in most of the beverages he prepared. I've included some of my grandmother's corn recipes passed down through many generations, but I dare not offer the recipes for my grandpa's corn beverages. For those, you will have to ask my brother Orestus.

THE RECIPES

Fried Fresh Corn
Batter-Fried Corn on the Cob
Pan-Fried Cornmeal Mush
Fresh Corn and Tomato Stew
Corncob Jelly

FRIED FRESH CORN
Serves 4

I think field corn is the very best for this dish, but you can use any other variety of sweet corn just as well. As you cut the kernels off the ears, be sure that you scrape the cobs to extract the milky juice with all that corn flavor.

6 ears yellow or white corn, shucked and silked
2 tablespoons butter
½ teaspoon salt, or to taste
¼ teaspoon freshly ground black pepper, or to taste
2 teaspoons sugar
Milk if needed

1. Using a sharp paring knife, cut the kernels from the corncob. After the kernels have been removed, scrape downward on the cob and collect all the milky liquid.

2. In a heavy 9-inch skillet, melt the butter over medium heat. Add the kernels and corn juice, sprinkle with the salt, pepper, and sugar, and cook, stirring frequently, for 10 to 15 minutes or until tender and thickened. If the corn starts to stick to the skillet, add a little milk. Serve immediately.

BATTER-FRIED CORN ON THE COB
Serves 6

Before we had a freezer, we used to can all our favorite vegetables, including corn *still on the cob*. Wide-mouthed half-gallon Ball Mason jars were used, and it was surprising how many ears of corn we could squeeze into them. A good thing, too, because this dish was a must for corn-shucking suppers, and with the canned ears, we always had enough to go around.

**6 ears fresh corn, shucked, silked, and cut in half crosswise
(thawed frozen ears can also be used)
¾ cup yellow cornmeal
⅓ cup all-purpose flour
½ teaspoon garlic salt (optional)
¾ cup milk
2 tablespoons plus 1 cup vegetable oil
1 large egg
1 cup cornflake crumbs**

1. In a medium bowl, combine the cornmeal, flour, garlic salt (if desired), milk, 2 tablespoons oil, and the egg. Mix well.

2. Place the cornflake crumbs in a shallow dish. Dip the halved ears of corn into the cornmeal batter to coat, then roll them in the cornflake crumbs.

3. In a deep fryer or heavy skillet, heat 1 cup oil over medium-high heat until hot but not smoking.

4. Fry the coated corn in the hot oil for 2 to 3 minutes or until light golden-brown. Place on heavy brown paper or paper towels to drain. Serve as soon as they are drained.

PAN-FRIED CORNMEAL MUSH
Serves 8 to 10

Once a mainstay of Southern country cuisine, cornmeal mush is simply coarsely ground yellow cornmeal slow cooked in water, stock, or milk while constantly stirred. This process transforms the cornmeal into a golden pudding.

The yellow corn used by our family for cornmeal mush was shucked and taken to the mill for grinding as soon as it was harvested. When it came back from the mill, the coarsely ground meal was stored in a tightly covered five-gallon tin bucket in the pantry, ready to be made into mush at any time. We ate it hot from the saucepan as a hearty breakfast, or cooked it with cracked black pepper as a side dish at other meals. Sometimes it was chilled, sliced, and then pan fried, and the crisp, brown outside contrasted with the creamy inside.

When I give this recipe to someone from the North, I call it *polenta*, which is what the Italians call cornmeal mush. If you want to call it *polenta*, too, mix in a quarter cup of grated Parmesan cheese at the end of the stirring time, or serve the pan-fried version with tomato sauce or salsa (which we, of course, call "relish"). I've even heard some of my customers say that it's great with crumbled goat cheese (which some of them call *"chevre"*).

6 ½ cups water
2 teaspoons salt, or to taste
2 cups coarsely ground yellow cornmeal
¼ cup butter, cubed
⅓ cup butter or vegetable oil

1. In a heavy saucepan, bring the water to a boil over high heat. Add the salt, reduce the heat to low, and very, very slowly add the cornmeal in a steady stream while stirring constantly with a wooden spoon. After adding all the cornmeal, reduce the heat until the mixture is just barely bubbling.

2. Continue cooking, stirring constantly, for 20 to 25 minutes or until the mixture is thickened and very smooth. When it is ready, the cornmeal will start to come away from the sides of the pan. Remove from heat, add the butter cubes, and stir until the butter is melted. (Note: At this point, the mush may be served as a breakfast porridge or as a side dish at other meals.)

3. Spread the cooked mush in a lightly greased shallow baking pan so that it forms a layer about ¾ inch thick. Cover and refrigerate for at least 2 hours.

4. Cut the chilled mush into 3 ½-inch squares. In a saute pan, heat the butter or oil over medium heat until hot but not smoking. Add as many squares of mush as you can fit in a single layer and cook, turning once, until golden-brown on both sides, about 3 minutes per side. Serve hot, lightly sprinkled with freshly ground black pepper as a side dish or topped with butter and maple syrup or molasses as a breakfast treat.

FRESH CORN AND TOMATO STEW
Serves 4

This is an easy version of a famous down-home food. The way it came about is not hard to figure out: at harvest time you have corn and you have tomatoes, so you cook them together in a skillet. Easy enough, but what a wonderful taste! Northerners may want to add a bit of chopped fresh cilantro to this dish.

3 ears fresh corn
3 ripe fresh tomatoes (about 1 ½ pounds)
1 cup fresh okra
1 tablespoon butter
¼ cup chopped green onion (including green part)
1 clove garlic, finely chopped
1 teaspoon salt, or to taste
½ teaspoon freshly ground black pepper, or to taste
1 teaspoon sugar
1 tablespoon minced fresh parsley, plus more for garnish if desired

1. Prepare the vegetables: cut the corn kernels from the cobs and scrape the corn milk from the cobs. Stem the tomatoes and cut them into small cubes. Wash the okra and thinly slice it. Set the vegetables aside.

2. In a heavy skillet, melt the butter over medium-high heat. Add the onions and garlic and saute until wilted, about 5 minutes, stirring occasionally. Add the corn, tomatoes, okra, and all remaining ingredients. Reduce heat to medium and cook, stirring frequently, for 10 minutes. Reduce heat to low, cover, and cook for 15 minutes more, stirring occasionally. Serve at once, garnished with additional parsley if desired.

CORNCOB JELLY
Makes about 1 ½ pints

If something *looks* as if it has no flavor, people tend to *think* it has no flavor. This almost colorless jelly can be made more appealing by adding a drop of yellow food coloring.

**12 ears fresh corn, preferably the limber cob variety,
shucked and silked, with kernels removed
4 cups water
4 cups sugar
3 ounces liquid fruit pectin
1 to 3 drops yellow food coloring (optional)**

1. Cut the bare corncobs into thirds, place in a large pot, and add the water. Bring to a boil over high heat, reduce heat to low, and simmer, covered, until the water is reduced to 3 cups, about 12 to 15 minutes.

2. Remove the corncobs and strain the remaining liquid through cheesecloth into a heavy 3-quart saucepan. If there is less than 3 cups of liquid, add water to make up the difference. Add the sugar and bring to a boil over high heat, stirring to dissolve the sugar. When the sugar is dissolved, add the pectin and, if desired, the food coloring, and cook for 1 minute longer.

3. Remove from heat, skim off any corn bits on the surface, and pour the jelly into hot, sterilized Ball Mason jars. Wipe the rims with a clean, damp towel, fit with hot lids, and tightly screw on the metal rings. Process the jars in a bath of boiling water, making sure that the jars are covered to a depth of 1 inch. Boil for 15 to 20 minutes, counting from when the water returns to a rapid boil after immersing the jars. Transfer the jars to a countertop to cool.

Seed-Ordering Day

When the seed catalogs arrive each winter in all their glossy glory, flaunting luscious red tomatoes and other dew-laden fruits and vegetables on every page, we forget it's the year we had decided to stop farming altogether. Before we know it, someone has planned a Seed-Ordering Day Dinner.

Now, this is a dinner for family members only. Anytime our family meets to discuss anything, it seems that we do it over food. But this is one time when I don't cook. I'm into seeds. I'm hooked on catalogs.

Before a roaring fire in the sitting room, we eat and talk about the upcoming farming season. Decisions are made about what to raise, how many acres to plant, whether we should bed our own sweet potatoes for plants or buy plants from a nearby farmer. Each of us also orders seeds from the catalogs for our personal kitchen, herb, and flower gardens. We don't share our thoughts on our personal ordering plans, but somehow we all seem to end up trying the very same new items featured in the catalogs.

In the comfort of fire and family, someone always reminisces about how special sitting in front of a wide, deep fireplace with a long hearth was for us in our childhood. And so, in taking our evening pleasure, just as in our farming and our cooking, the past is always part of our present.

CHAPTER 3

Starlight and Copper

My childhood days were filled with play, and also with my share of chores. One of those chores was minding my cow, Starlight. I don't know exactly what kind of cow she was, but she was spotted and she was definitely a milker. Our second milk cow was a Guernsey, but she was not in my care.

For me, milking was the most dreaded chore of all. My older sisters would say, "Boys don't like to hold hands with a girl who's been milking." And Lord knows, we had nothing in our house that could take that smell off your hands. You could use a little lilac dusting powder, or a drop of cheap perfume, but that was just a "covering over" smell. So I used deceit to get out of milking—I pretended my little fingers couldn't strip the milk from Starlight's bag.

But sometimes, as the years passed, no matter what, I would have to be the milker. When I was through, I would pick up the pail and carefully strain the milk, pouring it into large earthenware jugs. I would cover the mouths of the jugs with clean white cloth, which I tied fast with a string before replacing the lids. The jugs then had to be put in a warm spot. If it was winter, we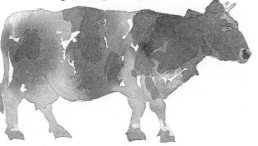

would set them near the fireplace so the warmth would help the milk clabber for churning.

Starlight's milk was always churned to make butter. Even then we never had very much, so we didn't eat food swimming in butter. Oh, yes, we ate rich food whenever company came, and always on Sunday. But during the week it was vegetables with just a little butter, if any at all.

We never drank sweet milk, either. Instead, we had buttermilk, the liquid left over from the milk after the butter was churned. I never could understand why they call it buttermilk, because when that churn was going, my mother got out every speck of butter. She would just churn and churn and churn until there was nothing left to rise to the top. Then she'd scoop, she'd skim, she'd stir, and she'd churn again to make sure that every drop of butter was out. In that house we didn't call it buttermilk, we called it butterless milk. For the first day after the churning, the butterless milk was very sweet and we would drink a bit as a kind of treat for breakfast, but any more than that and it would seem cloying. So we would wait two days until it had that tangy taste you get in buttermilk today. We used this gone-tangy buttermilk to make rich cornbread and fluffy mashed potatoes and wonderful desserts.

Even though I milked Starlight only once in a while, I always had to mind her. In the cool of summer mornings I would take her by the chain fastened to her neck halter and lead her to a grassy area on the farm. There she would graze on the dewladen wild grasses.

Sometimes there was good grazing near a tree stump or a bush where I could chain-fasten Starlight while gathering kudzu vines to make a jump rope. How I wished my cow liked kudzu. She didn't. But, oh, she loved the tender growing field corn, the wheat, the oats, the sugarcane, and the sorghum in our family's fields, and unfortunately for me, while I skipped rope among the kudzu, she sometimes pulled loose and strayed into those fields.

When the eleven o'clock freight train whistle blew, it was time for me to bring Starlight in to pasture. As we headed up the narrow dirt road toward the barn, Copper, my Rhode Island Red laying hen, would often meet us, eager for the corn kernels I scattered at the midday feeding. What a trio we made—a cow, a hen, and a little barefoot girl wearing a straw hat.

Gathering fresh eggs in the chicken house was easy, but not so for Copper's eggs. In a way, I think Copper had a little bantam hen mixed in her. Even though she was a Rhode Island Red, there was something just a little bit too wild about her. She frequently changed her nest, and often I had to listen for her cackling to lead me to the secret place where I could find her eggs. I always searched them out, though, because the eggs were mine—eggs to trade at the general store for candy, or a packaged cinnamon bun, or a Dixie cup of vanilla or strawberry ice cream with a little flat wooden spoon.

I remember all this so clearly, but I don't remember what happened to Starlight or even to Copper. I only know that suddenly they were no longer there. I suppose I have chosen to forget.

THE RECIPES

Fresh Eggs Baked with Grits and Ham
Eggs with Pan-Fried Bacon and Hominy
Fluffy Buttermilk Mashed Potatoes
Buttermilk Pralines
Buttermilk Pie with Raspberry Sauce
Buttermilk Ice Cream

FRESH EGGS BAKED WITH GRITS AND HAM
Serves 4

Here is a mouthwatering breakfast with all the ingredients in the same pot. It tastes best when made with country ham—slow-cured ham like the famous Smithfield hams from the Virginia county of the same name. Country hams are dry-cured, seasoned, smoked, and aged for months, and you can taste the care that goes into them. They can be ordered from any number of mail-order companies. If you can't get hold of country ham, you can use "regular" ham in this dish. You'll miss the smoky flavor, but a little fresh-ground pepper may help make up the difference.

About 4 cups cooled cooked grits
Salt to taste
2 eggs, lightly beaten
½ cup milk
¾ cup chopped cooked country ham
2 tablespoons butter
¼ cup shredded cheddar cheese

1. Preheat oven to 350° F.

2. If using regular grits, follow step 1 of the recipe for fried grits on page 187–88, but do not add the sugar and nutmeg. If using instant grits, prepare according to the directions on the package. In either case, once the grits are cooked, remove them from the heat and allow to cool about 3 minutes.

3. While the grits are cooling, combine the salt, eggs, milk, ham, butter, and cheese in a medium bowl and mix well.

4. Stir the egg-ham mixture into the cooled grits, mix well, then turn into a well-buttered 1 ½-quart casserole. Bake in the preheated oven for 30 to 35 minutes or until the top is lightly puffed. Allow to stand a few minutes before serving.

EGGS WITH PAN-FRIED BACON AND HOMINY

Serves 3

Hominy was long the backbone of rural cooking in the South. In the old days, dried corn kernels were cooked in a lye solution for about forty minutes, then steeped in the solution for about an hour more to loosen the hulls. The corn was then transferred to a large dishpan of clear water, the hulls removed by hand, and the kernels rinsed repeatedly until the water came clear and all the pieces of hull were gone. Today hominy is a food made easy—all you have to do is open a can.

6 slices meaty bacon
2 eggs, beaten
One 16-ounce can white hominy, drained
Salt and freshly ground black pepper to taste

1. In a heavy 12-inch skillet, fry the bacon over medium-high heat until crisp. Remove and drain on paper towels.

2. Pour off all but a thin layer of fat in the skillet. In a small bowl, combine the eggs and hominy and mix lightly. Pour the mixture into the hot skillet and scramble until done to your liking. Season to taste with salt and pepper. Serve with the drained bacon and hot biscuits (page 137–38).

FLUFFY BUTTERMILK MASHED POTATOES
Serves 4

If you want a bit of additional flavor in these delicious potatoes, mix in one or two finely chopped green onions just before serving.

1 ¼ pounds white boiling potatoes, peeled and sliced
1 teaspoon salt, or to taste
¾ cup warm buttermilk
½ teaspoon baking soda
2 teaspoons unsalted butter
Freshly ground black pepper to taste

1. Place the potatoes and salt in a medium saucepan and add enough water to cover. Bring to a boil over high heat. Reduce the heat and simmer until the potatoes are pierced easily with a fork, about 10 minutes. Drain, reserving a few tablespoons of the cooking liquid.

2. Place the potatoes in a large bowl and mash partially.

3. Add the warm buttermilk and baking soda, mix well, and mash completely. Stir in the butter and pepper and adjust the seasoning as needed. If you like your mashed potatoes creamy, add the reserved cooking liquid. Serve immediately.

BUTTERMILK PRALINES

Makes about 3 dozen whole pralines
or 5 cups crushed pralines

These sweet pralines—slightly tart from the buttermilk—can be eaten whole or crushed and sprinkled over ice cream.

3 cups sugar
1 cup buttermilk
1 teaspoon baking soda
¼ teaspoon salt
1 teaspoon vanilla extract
2 teaspoons butter
2 cups pecan halves

1. In a medium saucepan, mix together the sugar, buttermilk, baking soda, and salt. Cook over medium heat until a bit of the mixture forms a soft ball when dropped into cold water.

2. Remove from heat, stir in the vanilla, butter, and pecans, and return to heat. Cook, stirring constantly and scraping the bottom of the pan with your spoon, until the mixture again reaches the soft-ball stage. Remove from heat.

3. While still hot, drop mixture by the spoonful onto waxed paper. When cool, crush into bite-size pieces if desired or serve whole.

The Ice House

At family gatherings in the summer when I was a child, we always looked forward to fresh-churned, hand-cranked ice cream. The moment the ice cream was ready, it was put immediately into crushed ice that we fetched from the ice house out near the well. Before we had a real icebox, this was where we kept the ice.

Now, the ice house was not really a house at all. It was a small, round, rock- and straw-lined pit dug in the ground. The pit extended about three feet underground and at its bottom was a thick layer of sawdust.

Each Thursday morning when the ice truck came, you would have the iceman put a block of ice, maybe twenty-five pounds, into a burlap bag. Then you would get him to chop another block, maybe ten pounds, or five pounds, depending on how much money you had or what you had to barter.

That second block would go into another burlap bag. The bags would be lowered into the pit and other bags filled with sawdust would be set on top, and all of it covered over with a thick tin lid. Finally, a heavy rock was placed on top of the lid.

In this cool pit, ice would keep, even on the hottest summer days, for almost a week. We'd chip away at the blocks for ice to chill large tin buckets of lemonade and to freeze those wonderful hand-cranked churns of ice cream.

BUTTERMILK PIE WITH RASPBERRY SAUCE
Serves 6

This is a simple pie, but it is as delicate and delicious as any compli- cated dessert you'd find in a fancy restaurant. The raspberries cut the richness of the butter and sugar just a bit, so if you can't find rasp- berries, substitute another berry with some tartness, like blueberries or blackberries, rather than a sweeter berry, like strawberries.

4 tablespoons unsalted butter, softened

1 cup sugar

3 large eggs, lightly beaten

3 tablespoons all-purpose flour

1 teaspoon vanilla extract

2 tablespoons fresh lemon juice

1 cup buttermilk

A pinch of baking soda

1 unbaked 9-inch pie crust (page 81)

1 cup fresh raspberries or other tart berries

¼ cup black currant or other fruit liqueur

1. Preheat oven to 350° F.

2. In a medium bowl, combine the butter and sugar and beat until fluffy. Add the eggs one at a time, mixing well after each addition. Add the flour, vanilla, lemon juice, buttermilk, and baking soda and stir until well combined. Pour the mixture into the unbaked pastry shell.

3. Bake in the preheated oven for 15 minutes. Reduce heat to 300° F and bake for 1 hour more or until the custard is set and the top lightly browned. Remove from oven and place on a wire rack to cool.

4. Toss the raspberries with the black currant liqueur in a small bowl.

5. When the pie is cool enough to eat, cut it into slices and serve each slice topped with a generous spoonful of the raspberries.

BUTTERMILK ICE CREAM
Makes about 2 quarts

In our family, buttermilk ice cream is a tradition—one that I thought was unique until I went on a book tour and started talking about it. The very mention of buttermilk ice cream brought knowing nods, and recipes poured in, especially from the West.

In my family, it all started when my grandmother promised her children she would make a churn of hand-cranked ice cream if they found enough strawberries. A long search for the few remaining berries that season provided more than enough for ice cream. Looking at her children's faces, my grandmother didn't have the heart to tell them she'd forgotten her promise and traded away her raw sweet milk. And with the cow going dry, there probably would not be enough from the next milking to make ice cream either. So, knowing that fresh buttermilk is very mild and fairly sweet, Grandma churned clabber-ready milk into buttermilk. Using peach and strawberry jams to stretch her scant supply of sugar to sweeten the buttermilk, she made fresh wild strawberry ice cream. Today we still make it in much the same way, except we use an electric mixer and a newfangled ice cream maker to speed up the process.

1 ¼ cups sugar
½ cup water
¼ cup fresh lemon juice
¼ teaspoon cream of tartar
5 egg yolks
1 vanilla bean (you can substitute 1 teaspoon
vanilla extract)
3 cups buttermilk
1 quart fresh strawberries, washed and hulled
1 cup strawberry preserves

1. In a heavy saucepan, combine the sugar, water, lemon juice, and cream of tartar and mix well. Cook this mixture over moderately low heat, stirring constantly and washing down any sugar crystals that cling to the sides of the pan with a brush dipped in cold water, until the sugar is completely dissolved. Increase heat to high and boil the syrup until a candy thermometer registers 225° F.

2. In a large bowl, using an electric mixer, beat the egg yolks until they form a ribbon when the beater is lifted. Add the hot syrup in a stream while beating and continue to beat until the mixture is cool.

3. Halve the vanilla bean lengthwise and scrape the seeds into a medium bowl with the buttermilk. Mix together well and stir into the egg-and-syrup mixture.

4. Stir in the fresh strawberries and strawberry preserves, puree the mixture in a blender, and freeze in an ice cream maker according to the manufacturer's instructions.

CHAPTER 4

Hog-Killing Time

hen I was growing up, a lot of the meat we ate during the winter was wild game like venison and rabbit. Wild turkey and other game birds were also common. But the main meat on our table was pork.

Hog-killing time was a community event in Filbert, South Carolina, and it usually took place in December. December was colder back then, and it was important to kill the hogs on a cold day so the meat didn't have a chance to spoil. Cold weather was also important when preparing wild game for cooking. My father and older brother were hunters, and they made sure that venison was hung for several days before it was butchered for cooking, and rabbit for at least a day. Hanging game helps ensure tender meat, and the cold weather kept it from spoiling.

Some farmers argued that we should have the hog killing during a particular phase of the moon, but since there was an ongoing dispute about whether that meant when the moon was on the wax or when it was on the wane, the weather forecast in *The Farmer's Almanac* for the coldest day usually won out.

Butchering day involved a lot of work. In our family's log-cabin canning house, fresh sawdust was spread over the dirt floor. Hot-burning fires were built under the big, black cast-iron laundry pots, used not to boil clothes on butchering day

but to cook sausage and meat for canning and to make lard and crack-lings. Kerosene lanterns were hung from nails driven into the rafter beams over the long, wooden plank tables. Attached to either end of the tables were meat grinders with hand cranks to grind the sausage meat and the souse meat (what some people call hog's head cheese).

The work started in the very early morning hours and lasted well into the night. As soon as the spareribs had been removed from the hog car-cass and the meat used to make bacon became accessible, a narrow strip of the meat was sliced very thin, and several slits were made in the skin. Then it was seasoned with crumbled dried sage, salt, dried red pepper flakes, and black pepper and placed in a dish of buttermilk to marinate while we continued to work. The side meat used for bacon is quite fat but is also streaked with lean, so we called it "streaky lean."

The pig snouts were carefully cut and divided equally between two large pans. Since there was only one snout per pig and everyone wanted them, lots were cast to determine which cooks would have the privilege of making pickled pig lips. I have to tell you, though, that once a woman had enjoyed that privilege she gladly relinquished it to some other cook the next year, because pig lips are by no means easy to make.

In the late afternoon, the streaky-lean bacon slices, which had been marinating all day, were removed from the buttermilk, coated with a mixture of cornmeal and flour, and baked in a hot, hot oven until they were crispy brown. Then they were wedged between freshly baked but-termilk biscuits and served to the workers, along with hot sassafras tea served in speckled enameled tin cups and recycled tin cans.

I still have one of the big meat grinders that we used during hog killing, but these days I use it to make chowchow, a traditional cabbage relish. Like many other events, hog killings seem to be a thing of the past in York County, South Carolina.

THE RECIPES

Batter-Fried Country Ham Bites
Peachy Barbecued Spareribs
Pickled Pig Lips
Herb-Marinated Fried Rabbit
Braised Venison Steak
Buttermilk-Marinated Wild Turkey with Peppery Milk Gravy

BATTER-FRIED COUNTRY HAM BITES

Makes about 2 dozen

Appetizers are something I don't do much. The way I figure it, if we're going to eat, let's go straight to the meal. But if you come in totally famished and the pot's not finished boiling, I just might rustle up a few country ham bites to tide you over.

½ to 1 pound country ham (page 36), very thinly sliced
¾ cup all-purpose flour
¾ teaspoon baking powder
1 small egg
1 tablespoon milk
About 1 tablespoon water
About ¼ cup vegetable oil for skillet frying

1. Using a sharp knife, cut the ham slices into ¾" x 2" strips. Set aside.

2. In a small bowl, combine the flour and baking powder and mix well. In another small bowl, combine the egg and milk and mix well. Stir the egg mixture into the dry ingredients, adding enough water to make a batter that is quite thick, almost like a soft dough. Set aside.

3. In a medium skillet, heat the oil over medium-high heat until hot but not smoking.

4. Use your fingers to dredge the ham strips in the batter, coating the strips well. Place 2 or 3 strips on a slotted spatula and gently ease them into the hot oil. Add as many strips as you can without crowding the skillet. Cook, turning once, until golden-brown on both sides, about 5 to 6 minutes. Drain on paper towel. Continue to fry ham in batches until all the strips have been cooked. Serve immediately.

PEACHY BARBECUED SPARERIBS
Serves 6 to 8

Fresh summer peaches give pork a rich, fruity flavor and make a common meat special.

8 to 9 pounds spareribs in slab form, unseparated
⅓ cup fresh lemon juice
2 teaspoons paprika
4 to 5 fresh, ripe medium peaches, pureed in a food processor or
diced and mashed (about 2 cups)
1 medium onion, finely minced
½ teaspoon freshly ground black pepper, or to taste

For the barbecue sauce:

1 medium onion, finely minced
1 tablespoon vegetable oil
1 ½ cups ketchup
⅓ cup dark brown sugar
¼ cup cider vinegar
¼ teaspoon cayenne pepper, or to taste
1 tablespoon Worcestershire sauce

1. Wipe spareribs with damp paper towels and place them in a large roasting pan.

2. In a medium bowl, combine the lemon juice, paprika, peaches, onion, and black pepper and mix well. Spoon this marinade over the ribs, turning to coat well. Cover the pan and refrigerate overnight, turning the ribs occasionally.

3. In the morning, preheat the oven to 350° F. Remove the ribs from the marinade and drain the marinade into a medium saucepan. Set saucepan aside.

4. Place a roasting rack (use cake cooling racks if necessary) inside a large roasting pan. Place the ribs in a single layer, fat side up, on top of the rack and bake in the preheated oven for 1 ½ hours. Remove and allow the ribs to cool on a rack.

5. For the barbecue sauce, add the onion, vegetable oil, ketchup, brown sugar, vinegar, cayenne pepper, and Worcestershire sauce to the reserved marinade and mix well. Bring to a boil over high heat, stirring constantly. Immediately reduce the heat to low and simmer for 1 to 2 minutes, still stirring constantly. Remove from heat and set aside.

6. Cut the ribs into two-rib portions, drain the fat from the roasting pan, and place the ribs back in the pan. Pour the barbecue sauce over the ribs.

7. For final cooking in an oven: cover the pan with aluminum foil and bake at 350° F for 1 hour or until meat is tender.

For final cooking on a grill: remove the ribs from the pan, reserve the sauce, and cook the ribs over a medium-hot charcoal fire, basting and turning occasionally, for about 40 minutes or until the meat is tender.

PICKLED PIG LIPS
Makes 3 to 4 pints

I sometimes smile when I think that the lowly pig may have been responsible for introducing humans to the highly prized delicacy known as truffles. If the story is true, and I tend to believe it is, then perhaps, just perhaps, pickled pig lips will be looked upon favorably.

There's a fair amount of work involved in this recipe, but that's usually the case when you take a neglected part of an animal and put it through enough cooking processes to turn it into a tender and delicious treat. You will know the snouts are cooked properly when they attain the consistency of tender chicken gizzards.

3 to 4 pounds whole pig snouts
¼ cup pickling (kosher) salt
2 tablespoons pickling spices
1 teaspoon sugar
3 bay leaves
6 large cloves garlic
1 quart water
4 cups white distilled vinegar
1 teaspoon caraway seeds

1. Thoroughly wash the pig snouts and scrape them well to remove all hair. Place the snouts in a large stone crock.

2. In a medium saucepan, combine the pickling salt, pickling spices, sugar, bay leaves, garlic, and water. Bring to a boil over high heat and then pour into the crock. If necessary, add additional boiling water to cover the snouts completely.

3. Weight down the meat with a heavy bowl or plate topped by a clean brick or other heavy object. Cover the crock with cheesecloth, tie the cheesecloth tightly into place, then cover the cheesecloth with aluminum foil. Set the crock in a cool place and allow to stand for 10 days.

4. Drain the snouts, rinse well, and chop roughly. Place in a heavy 2-quart saucepan and cover with cold water. Add the vinegar and bring to a boil over high heat. Remove from heat briefly to skim the top of the liquid until the liquid is clear.

5. Reduce the heat to low, return the saucepan to the heat, add the caraway seeds, and simmer for 50 to 55 minutes or until the snout pieces are tender. Spoon the meat into hot, sterilized Ball Mason jars, leaving a ¼-inch space at the top of each jar. Wipe the jar rims with a clean, damp cloth, fit them with hot lids, and tightly screw on the metal rings.

Process in a bath of boiling water for five minutes (the water should cover the jars by about 1 inch), cool on a wire rack, and store in a cool, dark place.

The Cookstove

The top of the wood-burning iron cookstove in our old family home was a smooth surface with four recessed iron lids. Each lid was notched and there was a little iron handle that fit into the notch so you could lift the lid when you needed to stoke the fire.

The two burners in the bottom right-hand corner were the hottest ones, because the fire was directly underneath them. If you wanted to increase the heat under what you were cooking, you would just slide the pan over to one of those burners. If you wanted less heat, you would slide the pan across the stove to a cooler burner. The sound of pans sliding across that iron surface is one of my clearest childhood memories.

If you wanted to remove something from direct heat but needed to keep it warm, you had two choices. You could move it over on top of the water reservoir at the side of the stove, which was where we got our hot water, and the water simmering in the reservoir would keep the food warm; or you could move the pan to the warmers—shelves a bit above the back of the stovetop. The warmers were always used for bread while it was rising and to keep a dish warm while the rest of a meal was cooked.

I know it was old-fashioned, but I do believe that cookstove was more suited to family cooking than any modern stove I've ever seen.

HERB-MARINATED FRIED RABBIT
Serves 4 to 6

We used this recipe to cook wild rabbits when I was a child, but it works just as well for rabbits you buy in a store. They have a bit less flavor than the wild ones, but they make up for it by being more tender.

1 rabbit, 3 to 3 ½ pounds, cleaned and cut into pieces
¼ cup dry white wine
½ cup olive oil
1 tablespoon minced garlic
1 tablespoon dried parsley flakes
1 tablespoon dried sage
1 teaspoon salt, or to taste
1 teaspoon freshly ground black pepper, or to taste
¾ cup all-purpose flour
About 1 cup vegetable oil for skillet frying

1. Wash rabbit well, dry, and place in a 9" x 9" glass baking dish. In a small bowl, combine the wine, olive oil, garlic, parsley, sage, salt, and pepper. Mix well and pour over rabbit. Let stand at room temperature for 1 hour, turning a few times.

2. Place the flour in a shallow baking dish. Remove the rabbit from the marinade and place on paper towels to drain.

3. Pour enough of the vegetable oil into a 10-inch skillet to come to a depth of about ¼ inch and heat over medium-high heat until hot but not smoking.

4. Dredge the rabbit in the flour one piece at a time, coating evenly. Place in the skillet in a single layer (in two batches, if necessary) and cook until browned on all sides, about 4 minutes per side. Remove from the skillet and set aside.

5. With a large metal spoon or a baster, remove as much oil from the skillet as possible. Return the rabbit to the skillet, reduce heat to medium-low, cover, and cook the rabbit in its own juices until the meat is tender and no longer pink near the bone, about 15 to 20 minutes. Remove lid and raise heat to high for 1 to 2 minutes, if desired, to make the skin crispy. Serve at once.

BRAISED VENISON STEAK
Serves 4 to 6

Because venison is so lean, I have found it adapts well to long, slow, moist cooking methods such as braising or stewing. In this recipe, the meat is first marinated in buttermilk to tenderize it and to tame the gamy taste a bit, then browned in bacon fat, and finally slowly braised. Cooked this way, the venison is very tender and goes well with country-style turnip greens (page 89–90) and sweet potato rolls (page 126–27).

2 pounds venison steak
2 cups buttermilk
1 teaspoon salt
½ teaspoon freshly ground black pepper
½ teaspoon dried sage (1 teaspoon minced fresh)
¼ pound bacon
¼ cup boiling water

1. Cut the venison steak into thin slices. Place in a medium glass casserole dish, add the buttermilk, and turn to coat well. Cover and refrigerate overnight, turning the meat several times.

2. Drain the meat thoroughly and discard the marinade. Rub the steaks with salt, pepper, and sage and set aside.

3. In a deep skillet, brown the bacon over medium-high heat. Place the bacon on paper towels to drain and remove all but two tablespoons of the fat from the skillet.

4. Place the venison slices in the skillet and brown over medium-high heat, 2 to 3 minutes per side. Return the drained bacon to the skillet along with the boiling water. Reduce heat to low, cover, and cook for about 30 minutes or until meat is tender.

BUTTERMILK-MARINATED WILD TURKEY
WITH PEPPERY MILK GRAVY
Serves 15 to 20

The berries and grains that wild turkeys feed on produce a different taste from that of the tended flock fed on commercial grains. The wild turkey's active lifestyle—searching for food and running to escape capture—also makes for a much leaner bird. In this recipe, I use a bread and sherry stuffing to pull some of the wild, gamy taste out of the bird. After the turkey is cooked, the stuffing is discarded. This is a forerunner of today's stuffings, which are meant to be eaten.

If you can't get hold of a wild turkey, you can use a domesticated bird for this recipe.

1 wild turkey, 13 to 15 pounds, plucked and drawn
Salt and freshly ground black pepper to taste
2 quarts buttermilk
1 cup chopped onion
1 cup chopped celery
2 teaspoons paprika
2 slices white bread, torn into small pieces
1 ½ cups sherry
1 tablespoon butter, melted

1. Wash and dry the turkey and sprinkle with salt and pepper inside and out. Place in a large, deep roasting pan, pour the buttermilk over the top, and marinate overnight, turning several times.

2. Remove the turkey from the marinade, drain, discard any remaining marinade, and place the turkey in a shallow roasting pan.

3. Preheat oven to 350° F. In a small bowl, combine the onion, celery, paprika, bread, and 1 cup of the sherry and mix well. Stuff the turkey with this mixture. Dip a clean cloth into the melted butter and rub the entire exterior of the turkey with it.

4. Place turkey in preheated oven and roast, basting with pan drippings and the remaining ½ cup of sherry every 15 to 20 minutes, for approximately 20 minutes per pound or until the juices run clear when the thigh is deeply pierced. Remove turkey from oven, remove and discard stuffing (it is not meant to be eaten), and carve. Serve with peppery milk gravy (page 57).

PEPPERY MILK GRAVY

Makes about 2 cups

Be generous with the pepper here; it really adds to the flavor. Don't forget that gravy thickens as it cools. If the gravy becomes too thick, add a little hot water and reheat, stirring constantly.

¼ cup pan drippings from the turkey
¼ cup all-purpose flour
2 cups milk
Salt to taste
Freshly ground black pepper to taste

1. Pour out all but about ¼ cup of the drippings from the turkey pan. Over a burner set on low, add the flour to the remaining drippings and stir to make a smooth paste. Cook, stirring constantly, until the mixture begins to bubble.

2. Remove from heat and stir in the milk in three parts, mixing after each addition until smooth. Return to heat and cook, stirring constantly, until the mixture thickens. Add salt and pepper to taste and serve at once.

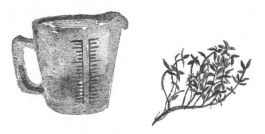

Stretching the Meat

Since the very earliest days, we African-Americans have had to learn how to stretch expensive ingredients. We did it out of necessity but ended up with many wonderful foods as a result. That's where chitterlings (say it "chitlins") came from, and today I make what I call chicken cracklings.

They're very easy. You just take well-seasoned chicken skins and put them in the oven at a very, very high heat, watching carefully so that they don't burn. As soon as the chicken skin is brown and crispy, which doesn't take long because the heat is so high, remove and set them aside. After the skins have cooled, you break them into little pieces. Then you take these bits of crispy skin and stir them into fresh, hot mashed potatoes. For those of you who can abide just a trace of fat, this is the most delicious thing you can imagine— and that's what we call stretching the meat.

CHAPTER 5

Making Molasses

I n the old days, when the crops had been harvested, the fields were opened up to the children for gleaning. On our farm, sweet potato gleaning was the best. Usually many potatoes were left in the ground. My father would include our gleanings in his sales, but the money would be ours to keep.

Since Hurricane Hugo hit our area in 1989, I have returned to the practice of gleaning. Even after we close our farm stand in September, there is still fruit and other produce in the orchards and fields. When the last peaches are picked from the trees, there are no more until the next spring, but late-summer crowder peas, okra, tomatoes, peppers, and some other vegetables continue to bear until the first frost. I pick and can everything I find, determined to be prepared if another hurricane blows up the coast to Carolina.

Later in the fall, I'll join Miss Hattie Fay, a longtime friend, to pick muscadine grapes for jellies and pies. After the second frost we will gather wild persimmons (they're sweeter then) for jams, puddings, and persimmon beer.

These post-harvest activities always bring back memories of autumn events in years gone by—corn-shucking suppers, fundraising box suppers, and a very, very special time—molasses-making days. Even when I am away from the farm at molasses-making time, my thoughts still swirl around those crisp fall mornings of my childhood when the molasses mill that my father owned and operated with my mother's help was in full swing.

The local farmers and their wives would arrive at the crack of dawn in wagons loaded with fodder-free sugarcane stalks that they had cut and stripped the day before. They also brought new tin buckets for the molasses and baskets of food still warm from the oven. What heavenly smells — the women must have cooked all night.

The menfolk took turns hand-feeding the cane stalks into the mule-driven mill. During the course of the day, several mules would take turns walking in a circle pressing out the juice. Maude and Daisy, our family's mules, seemed to me to be the best workers. As the mules walked round and round, the sweet juice flowed out of the press through clean pipes into a long, heavy steel evaporator pan positioned over a brick oven. The raw sugarcane juice was then cooked down over a constant high heat that turned it into delicious molasses.

A completely cooked vat of cane juice converted to molasses was called a "run," because it was ready to run off into the gallon, half-gallon, and quart buckets that the folks had brought. There were always a few runs that were slightly overcooked, not as tasty as the others, and therefore difficult to sell. One of these runs was set aside to make into brown sugar for holiday baking the following year. That was another uniquely Southern tradition.

Here's how it worked: the syrup from the "dark" run was stored through the winter in tightly covered five-gallon galvanized tin containers. Then, on hot, dry days during late spring and summer, the lids were removed, the syrup stirred with clean, bark-stripped gum tree wood sticks, and the lids replaced by fine screen wire or cheesecloth to allow the drying process. By early fall there was usually only a thin layer of syrup left on top. The rest had become darkly sweet unrefined brown sugar, used in pecan pies, caramel icings, fruitcakes, and other wonderful holiday desserts.

Making molasses was a barter arrangement between my parents and the other local farmers. No money changed hands around the press. Instead, my parents made the molasses for a share of the total yield. Any molasses that was not needed by our family was sold, and my siblings and I made molasses candy to sell, too.

A local Filbert, South Carolina, farmer, an old family friend, still makes molasses using pretty much the same method. His sugarcane press is powered by electricity instead of mules, but that's about the only difference. He even uses the same barter system. It's good to see that some things don't change all that easily.

THE RECIPES

Grandma's Coffee Can Molasses Bread
Ginger Molasses Cookies
Crybaby Cookies
Johnnycakes

GRANDMA'S COFFEE CAN MOLASSES BREAD
Makes two 1-pound loaves

There are many stories in our family about how this simple, dense, and delicious bread was invented. My favorite is my grandmother's. "One day when I was baking," she used to say, "I found that my oven was completely full, except for two little spaces in the corners. The only thing that could fit in there was a coffee can, so I figured I would make my molasses bread that way." We've been making it like that in our family ever since.

2 cups whole wheat flour
½ cup fine-grind white cornmeal
2 teaspoons baking soda
½ teaspoon salt
2 cups buttermilk
½ cup molasses
½ cup seedless raisins
½ cup finely chopped dried apples

1. Preheat oven to 350° F. In a large bowl, combine all the ingredients and mix well.

2. Spoon the batter into 2 well-greased and floured coffee cans. Allow to stand for 30 minutes.

3. Bake in the preheated oven for 50 to 55 minutes or until the top is golden and a knife inserted in the center of the bread comes out clean.

Cool on a wire rack for 10 minutes, then run a knife around the edges of the coffee cans, gently remove bread, and cool completely.

GINGER MOLASSES COOKIES
Makes about 24 cookies

These simple cookies, rich with thick molasses and aromatic spices, were always made for holidays and special occasions when I was a child.

¾ cup shortening
1 cup sugar
¼ cup molasses
1 large egg
2 cups all-purpose flour
⅛ teaspoon salt
2 teaspoons baking soda
1 teaspoon ground ginger
½ teaspoon ground cloves
½ teaspoon ground nutmeg
1 teaspoon ground cinnamon

1. Preheat oven to 350° F. In a medium bowl, cream the shortening and sugar, beating until light and fluffy. Add the molasses and egg and beat until well combined. Add all the remaining ingredients and again beat until well combined.

2. Shape the dough into walnut-size balls and place on ungreased baking sheets. Flatten balls with a lightly floured hand. Bake for 12 to

15 minutes or until the cookies are golden. Remove from sheets with a spatula and cool on wire racks.

CRYBABY COOKIES
Makes 6 to 8 dozen

Here it is, the famous cookie you give to a crying baby to make it happy again. At molasses-making time we made these cookies by the dozens, but there were never enough left over to sell—they made us all so happy we couldn't resist them.

1 cup sugar
¼ cup butter
2 eggs, lightly beaten
1 cup molasses
1 cup milk
4 cups all-purpose flour
2 teaspoons baking soda
¼ teaspoon each: ground nutmeg, ground cloves, allspice
¼ teaspoon ground ginger
1 teaspoon ground cinnamon
1 cup seedless raisins, tossed with 2 tablespoons all-purpose flour

1. Preheat oven to 350° F. In a large bowl, cream the sugar and butter, beating until light and fluffy. Add the eggs, then the molasses, then the milk, beating after each addition until well combined.

2. In another large bowl, sift together the flour, the baking soda, and all the spices. Add to the butter-egg mixture in thirds, beating after each addition just until well mixed. Gently stir in the raisins.

3. Drop the batter by scant tablespoons onto greased cookie sheets. Bake in the preheated oven for 10 to 12 minutes or until golden-brown. Remove with a spatula, cool on wire racks, and feed to babies or guests.

JOHNNYCAKES
Serves 4

These traditional Southern pancakes were a favorite autumn dish, served at family breakfasts as soon as molasses was made. Today they remain a delicious breakfast treat.

1 cup fine white cornmeal
1 tablespoon light or dark brown sugar
¼ teaspoon salt
About 4 tablespoons milk
1 tablespoon butter, melted
1 tablespoon vegetable oil for the griddle

1. In a large bowl, combine the cornmeal, brown sugar, and salt with enough boiling water to make a batter just slightly thinner than mashed potatoes. Stir in the milk and butter.

2. Heat the oil on the griddle over medium-high heat until hot but not smoking. Drop the batter by spoonfuls onto the griddle and fry, turning once, until both sides of the cake are well browned, about 3 to 5 minutes per side. Serve with fresh molasses and butter for breakfast, or plain any time of day.

Wild Persimmon Beer

Wild persimmon beer was made in the fall, but preparations started long before that. Besides persimmons, the other main ingredients in this potion were wild honey locust pods, which—like the persimmons—ripened in the fall, and clear, pure rainwater. Just in case a dry spell came along, we started collecting the water in late summer. Every time it rained, we would set out one-gallon clear glass jugs that originally held Coca-Cola syrup (we got them from the drugstore in town). Of course, it usually rained again before the collected water was actually needed, so the old stored water was replaced by freshly caught water.

After the first heavy frost, we started gathering the honey locust pods and the wild persimmons, which by then had become sweet. A few shakes of the usually small-trunked persimmon trees would knock down any fruit still clinging to the branches. We picked up bucketfuls, then carefully picked them over. The sound ones were washed, their caps removed, then lightly mashed in a large bowl. The honey locust pods we gathered were also checked over, the sound ones rinsed, drained, and broken into pieces.

In the bottom of a clean stone crock or a wooden keg (my father had one with a spigot), we placed a layer of freshly ground coarse cornmeal. Next came a layer of honey locust pods and then a layer of wild persimmons. The layers were repeated until they reached about three inches from the top of the container, ending with a top layer of cornmeal. Finally the crock or keg was filled with just enough rainwater to cover the final layer completely, the lid put on, and the mixture left to ferment. When Aunt Vestula visited, she would decide when the beer was ready to drink. It was supposed to be for adults only, but she would always slip us children just a little taste. I remember it as sweet and musty, tasting more of persimmon and locust than alcohol.

CHAPTER 6

Picking Peaches

When I was a child, there were peach orchards on either side of the long road that led to our farmhouse. On the left side of that road was a narrow path that wound down through the peach trees to a little open patch of land. There one of my older sisters had a small garden where she raised vegetables that won the 4-H contest almost every year.

Along the right-hand side of that little path leading to the garden were about twenty-five peach trees that bore yellow-fleshed freestone peaches. Those peaches were the best I've ever tasted. The juicy flesh was a beautiful golden color and the taste was sweet as honey, mellow but intense.

Although I have yet to find peaches today that taste so perfect, those that come closest are our Sunhigh peaches. They are my very favorite of the modern peaches and we have about an acre of them on our farm.

When I am selling fruits and vegetables at the farm stand, I always have some Sunhighs ready for tasting, along with lots of paper towels. I've never had a customer taste a Sunhigh and go away without buying some. Sometimes customers drive up with peaches in the back of their car that they bought elsewhere and they say, "We don't need any more peaches today." Well, I just say, "But what about a Sunhigh?"—and don't you know, when they leave they have a basket of Sunhighs with them.

Of course, we raise many other kinds of peaches, too. That way, we have peaches ripening from the end of June, when we first open the farm stand for the season, all the way through the summer. My brother Orestus has a little cardboard that he tacks up at the farm stand with tenpenny nails on which he posts the date he is going to start picking certain varieties of peaches, so people will know when to come. The sign will say, "Georgia Belle peach picking will begin about July 21. You will be able to expect Alberta peaches the first week of August."

The schedule is pretty much the same from year to year. The first to ripen are the clingstone and semi-cling peaches, so called because the flesh clings to the pit. These are used mostly for eating out of hand, for making ice cream and cobblers, and for pickling. Next come the free-stone peaches, which begin to ripen in July. Because the flesh practically falls away from the pit when cut, these peaches slice wonderfully, and to my taste they have more flavor than the cling varieties. White-fleshed Early Georgia Belles are usually ripe then, too. Later in the month you get regular Georgia Belles and a large variety of yellow-fleshed peaches, like Albertas, Blakes, Redskins, Monroes, and, of course, Sunhighs.

The schedule can change completely, though, if there is a lot of rain. Rain tends to ripen peaches more quickly, but it also takes away their taste. It makes them more watery-bland. When the weather is dry, you get peaches with an intense flavor, almost as if they are sun-dried. As we like to say, "The drier the weather, the sweeter the peach."

Though most farmers now have irrigation, we still don't, so sometimes during a dry season the peaches are smaller—but, oh, their flavor is wonderful.

I still pick peaches almost every day during the summer. I try not to be too choosy about most things in life, but with my peaches I am as choosy as can be. Because of this, I try to keep two of my brothers out of the orchard. Both of them are color-blind, one more so than the other, and they can't really tell when the peaches are properly ripe. When peaches are at their peak they have that wonderful blush-orangy glow. Or, if they are white peaches like Georgia Belles, they are a creamy white on one side with a blush of red on the other.

Really, not much has changed in our orchards since my childhood, when I used to walk barefoot down that little path. When the peaches are truly ripe, the air in the orchard is perfumed with their fragrance and they lure me to them once again. I always think maybe, just maybe, this will be the day I pick a Sunhigh that tastes exactly like those peaches I ate in the sunny orchard by my sister's garden.

THE RECIPES

Bourbon-Laced Tipsy Chicken with Peaches
Peach Salad
Peach Cornmeal Muffins
Farm Stand Peach Jam
Cantaloupe-Peach Conserve with Pecans
Peach-Nutmeg Custard
Easy Peach Cobbler
Fresh Peach Pie

Flash Freezing Peaches

Unless my brothers picked them, my peaches don't have stems on them when they come off the tree. The presence of a stem indicates that the peach was pulled before it had ripened. My peaches have a slight opening where they have been ever so gently pulled from the stem. Water can seep into that opening if you put the peaches to soak, so I never do that. I just run my peaches under water and dry them off. Sometimes I don't peel my peaches before freezing them, because the skin adds flavor. I simply slice the washed peaches, put the slices from one or two peaches directly into a little plastic bag along with just a trace of sugar to keep the color, then seal the bag and freeze it right away. That is what I call flash freezing peaches. When you thaw them, they still have that wonderful fresh peach color and flavor.

BOURBON-LACED TIPSY CHICKEN WITH PEACHES

Serves 4

This was one of my Aunt Vestula's favorite recipes. Oh, she did like to cook with wine and spirits.

4 chicken leg quarters (thigh attached)
½ teaspoon salt, or to taste
⅛ teaspoon freshly ground black pepper, or to taste
2 tablespoons butter
1 large onion, finely chopped
1 teaspoon paprika
1 ½ cups green onions, chopped (about 6 green onions,
including green part)
½ cup orange juice
2 tablespoons bourbon
1 cup chopped fresh peaches (about 2 medium peaches)
A dash of nutmeg

1. Preheat oven to 400° F.

2. Sprinkle chicken quarters with salt and pepper. Place in a 13" x 9" baking pan and set aside.

3. In a medium skillet, melt the butter over medium heat. Add the chopped onion and cook, stirring occasionally, until translucent, about 5 minutes. Add the paprika and all but 1 tablespoon of the green onions and continue to cook, stirring occasionally, for an additional 4 minutes.

4. Spread the onion mixture evenly over the chicken, spoon the orange juice and bourbon over the top, and bake in the preheated oven for 30 minutes, turning and basting occasionally.

5. Remove the chicken from the oven, spoon the peaches over the top, sprinkle with nutmeg, and return to the oven for an additional 15 to 20 minutes or until the chicken is tender and shows no trace of pink near the bone. Remove the chicken from the pan, place on a serving dish, and pour the pan juices over the chicken. Garnish with the remaining green onions and serve immediately.

PEACH SALAD
Serves 6

My mama sometimes served this salad with chicory, which she often wilted before adding to the salad. Whether or not she wilted the chicory, she always added a pinch or two of freshly grated nutmeg to the greens.

⅓ cup vegetable oil
⅓ cup red wine vinegar
2 cloves garlic, peeled and split
½ teaspoon sugar
½ teaspoon lemon pepper (you can substitute
freshly ground black pepper)
4 cups lettuce, torn
½ cup endive or chicory, cut into bite-size pieces
1 cup fresh peaches, cubed or sliced (about 2 medium peaches)
A generous pinch of freshly grated nutmeg

1. In a jar, combine the oil, vinegar, garlic, sugar, and pepper. Cover and shake well. Chill the dressing for several hours to blend flavors, then remove the garlic cloves.

2. In a large bowl, combine the lettuce, endive or chicory, peaches, and nutmeg. Pour dressing over the top, toss, and serve.

PEACH CORNMEAL MUFFINS
Makes 1 dozen

This is a peachy food to start the working day. Of course, a little bit of bacon and eggs and some country ham won't hurt, either.

½ cup butter
½ cup sugar
1 large egg
1 cup all-purpose flour
½ cup white cornmeal
⅛ teaspoon salt
1 ½ teaspoons baking powder
⅛ teaspoon ground nutmeg
½ cup milk
1 cup finely chopped fresh peaches
(about 2 medium peaches)

1. Preheat oven to 350° F.

2. In a large bowl, cream the butter and sugar, beating until light and fluffy. Add the egg and again beat until light and fluffy.

3. In a separate bowl, combine the flour, cornmeal, salt, baking powder, and nutmeg and mix well. Add this dry mixture to the butter mixture in two parts alternating with the milk, stirring after each addition until just combined. Add the fresh peaches and stir to blend.

4. Fill greased muffin tins two-thirds full with the batter and bake in the preheated oven for about 25 minutes or until golden. Cool for 5 minutes on a wire rack, then gently remove from muffin tins and allow to cool completely.

FARM STAND PEACH JAM

Makes about 3 pints

Yellow- or white-fleshed peaches can be used for this jam. Now that I've given you the recipe, I know I'll hear a lot of "Oh, I made ten quarts of your jam with white-fleshed peaches," and that will make me feel a little left behind, because these days I don't often have time to make jams and jellies. But you can always bring me a sample.

5 cups ripe fresh peaches (about 8 to 10 medium peaches),
peeled, pitted, and finely chopped
2 tablespoons fresh lemon juice
1 ¾ ounces powdered fruit pectin
3 ½ cups sugar
1 teaspoon butter, melted

1. In an 8-quart kettle, combine the peaches and lemon juice.

2. In a small bowl, combine the pectin and ¼ cup of the sugar and mix well. Stir into the peach mixture along with the butter.

3. Over medium-high heat, bring the peach mixture to a full boil, stirring constantly. Stir in the remaining 3 ¼ cups sugar, return the mixture to a full boil, and cook for 1 minute, stirring constantly.

4. Remove from heat, quickly skim off any foam, and ladle the jam at once into hot, sterilized Ball Mason jars, leaving a ¼-inch space at the top of each jar. Wipe the jar rims with a clean, damp cloth, fit them with hot lids, and tightly screw on the metal rings.

5. Process in a bath of boiling water for 5 minutes (water should cover the jars by about 1 inch), cool on a wire rack, and store in a cool, dry place.

CANTALOUPE-PEACH CONSERVE
WITH PECANS
Makes about 3 to 4 pints

This conserve is very pretty and has a unique flavor, so it makes a wonderful gift. For that reason, I usually put it up in half-pint jars. Just make sure the cantaloupes you use are not overripe or you will end up with cantaloupe soup.

1 medium cantaloupe (rind removed) seeded and diced
6 ripe medium peaches, peeled, pitted, and diced
2 medium oranges, peeled, seeds and pith removed,
and flesh cut into small chunks
½ cup sugar per cup of fruit (about 4 to 5 cups)
⅛ teaspoon salt
¼ cup chopped pecans

1. In a large saucepan, combine the cantaloupe, peaches, and oranges and mix well. Add water to cover the fruit by ¼ inch and bring to a boil over medium heat. Cook, stirring constantly, for 10 minutes. Remove from heat and measure mixture.

2. Return measured fruit to saucepan and add ½ cup of sugar for each cup of fruit. Stir in the salt, return to boil over medium heat, and cook, stirring occasionally, for 45 minutes to 1 hour or until the mixture has thickened.

3. Remove from heat, stir in pecans, and, while mixture is still hot, pour into sterilized jars. Wipe the jar rims clean with a damp towel and put on the lids.

4. Process in a bath of boiling water for 5 minutes (the water should cover the jars by about 1 inch), cool on a wire rack, and store in a cool, dark place.

PEACH-NUTMEG CUSTARD
Serves 6

Mama made this delicious dessert in the middle of winter using our own home-canned peaches. I do, too, when I take the time to can my own, but it tastes wonderful even if you use store-bought canned peaches.

One 20-ounce can peach halves in syrup, very well drained
1 ½ cups milk
1 large egg plus 4 large egg yolks
½ cup sugar, or to taste
½ teaspoon vanilla extract
½ teaspoon lemon extract
½ teaspoon ground nutmeg
1 tablespoon peach brandy (optional)

1. Preheat oven to 350° F.

2. Lightly butter a shallow ½-quart casserole dish. Arrange the peaches cut side up in the dish. Set aside.

3. In a medium saucepan, warm the milk over medium heat until tiny bubbles appear around the edges.

4. While the milk is warming, combine the egg, egg yolks, sugar, vanilla extract, lemon extract, nutmeg, and, if desired, the brandy in a small bowl and mix well. Add this mixture to the warm milk, stirring constantly.

5. Strain the milk-egg mixture over the peaches. Place the casserole dish inside a large roasting pan and add enough hot water to the roasting pan to reach halfway up the side of the casserole dish. Bake in the preheated oven for about 1 hour or until the top is golden and the custard is set. Serve warm or cold.

EASY PEACH COBBLER
Serves 6 to 8

As this cobbler bakes, the batter bubbles up through the peaches to form a crusty topping. For that reason, some cooks call it "miracle pie." Whatever you call it, it couldn't be easier.

½ cup unsalted butter, melted
1 cup all-purpose flour
1 ½ cups sugar, or to taste
3 teaspoons baking powder
A pinch of salt
1 cup milk
4 cups peeled, pitted, and thinly sliced fresh peaches
(5 to 6 medium peaches)
1 tablespoon fresh lemon juice
Several dashes ground cinnamon or ground nutmeg (optional)

1. Preheat oven to 375° F.
2. Pour the melted butter into a 13" x 9" x 2" baking dish.

3. In a medium bowl, combine the flour, 1 cup of the sugar, the baking powder, and the salt and mix well. Stir in the milk, mixing until just combined. Pour this batter over the butter but do not stir them together.

4. In a small saucepan, combine the peaches, lemon juice, and remaining cup of sugar and bring to a boil over high heat, stirring constantly. Pour the peaches over the batter but do not stir them together. Sprinkle with cinnamon or nutmeg if desired.

5. Bake in the preheated oven for 40 to 45 minutes or until the top is golden-brown. Serve warm or cold.

FRESH PEACH PIE

Makes one 9-inch pie

As soon as I spot a ripe Alberta peach in the orchard, I search to find enough to make a pie or two. This is a great recipe for company since it doubles easily.

3 pounds fresh, ripe peaches (about 7 medium peaches),
pitted, blanched, peeled, and sliced
2 tablespoons fresh lemon juice
¾ cup sugar, or to taste
2 tablespoons cornstarch
¼ teaspoon ground cinnamon
1 unbaked 9-inch pie shell plus top crust (page 81)

1. Preheat oven to 400° F.

2. In a large bowl, gently toss the peach slices with the lemon juice. Set aside.

3. In a small bowl, combine the sugar, cornstarch, and cinnamon and mix well. Add to the peaches, mix well, and pour into the pie shell.

4. Drape the pastry for the top crust over a floured rolling pin. Position the pastry over the pie and gently lay it on top of the filling, sliding the rolling pin from under the pastry. Trim the edges of the shell and top crust to ¾ inch, press the edges together lightly, fold under, and seal. Flute with fingers or crimp with a fork. With a paring knife, cut small slits near the center of the top crust for vents.

5. Bake on the center rack in the preheated oven for 20 minutes. Remove and cover edges of crust with foil. Return to oven and bake an additional 40 to 45 minutes or until well browned and bubbly. Cool completely on a wire rack before serving.

BEST-EVER PIE PASTRY
Makes two 9-inch crusts

2 ½ cups all-purpose flour
1 teaspoon salt
⅔ cup chilled shortening
¼ cup chilled unsalted butter, cut into small pieces
6 to 7 tablespoons ice water

1. In a medium bowl, sift together the flour and salt. Cut in the shortening and butter with a pastry blender until the mixture resembles coarse cornmeal. Sprinkle with ice water 1 tablespoon at a time, mixing with a fork, until the pastry just holds together to form a dough.

2. Divide the dough in half. Shape each half into a ball, enclose in plastic wrap, and refrigerate overnight or for at least 2 hours.

3. Remove dough from refrigerator. If it is very cold, allow to stand at room temperature for a few minutes before rolling. On a lightly floured surface, roll out the dough with a floured rolling pin to make a disk about 12 inches in diameter. Drape over the rolling pin and transfer to a 9-inch pie plate. Press pastry gently to line the pan but do not stretch it.

4. Reflour the rolling pin and the rolling surface and roll out the remaining dough to make another disk about 12 inches in diameter for the top crust. Proceed as directed in your particular pie recipe.

Nutmeg

When my Aunt Vestula came to visit, she brought new ideas with her that became part of our family cooking over the years. I don't know if they were just her own notions about what tasted good or the influence of the people for whom she cooked in the Low Country.

On one trip she taught my mother how to use nutmeg. Not the kind you buy in a box already ground, but the whole nutmeg that you grate yourself. When I was a child, we always had nutmeg in the house, even if we didn't have any other spices, and it was always being grated into all kinds of wonderful dishes. My mother would even put nutmeg on our meat. Just a pinch, though — it doesn't take much. The meat would take on that subtle flavor you sometimes get from paprika in goulash. It was so delicious, I still use nutmeg all the time in my own cooking. I like it with most every-thing, but to me it goes the very best with our wonderful peaches.

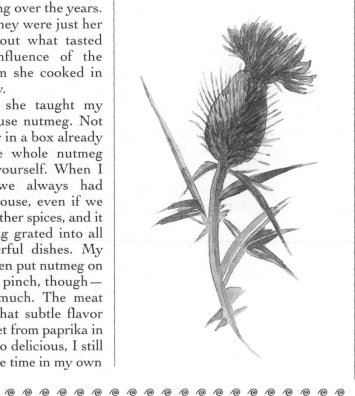

CHAPTER 7

Wild Spring Greens

armers eat what the seasons offer. Spring brings "splendor in the weeds" and memories of roaming the pastures with my mother and my siblings collecting "volunteer" wild greens—creasie greens, pokeweed, and dandelion greens.

Even now I still keep a watchful eye on the meadows for the first sign of the edibles. When the redbud and dogwood trees are in bloom and the fragrant smell of Carolina spice flowers fills the house, I know the time for picking wild mulberries is near. Within weeks, the blooming wild strawberries will be ready to pick and each day I will be able to gather a mess of field cress (one mess equals enough for a meal), the wild version of watercress that Carolinians call creasie greens.

Next come dandelions and pokeweed. It is often said that a meal or two of pokeweed salad will give the body a healthy boost for the hot summer months ahead. You can usually find pokeweed at the edges of fields or along the sides of old barns and other abandoned buildings. Right now I find some of my best pokeweed next to the old tractor shed on our family farm. But I also find it scattered throughout the orchard, or, for that matter, almost anywhere. Once it gets started it just spreads.

To me, pokeweed tastes much like green beet leaves but with a stronger flavor. Be sure to boil the poke before you use it; this helps tame its sometimes bitter taste. Always pick very, very young pokeweed, commonly called poke salad sprouts, if you can find it. I stop picking poke-weed to eat once the berries appear on the plant.

In my recipes, you can substitute other strong-flavored greens such as mustard greens if you can't find pokeweed. On the other hand, you might try becoming familiar with the flavor of wild American pokeweed and see how well it can substitute for other vegetables in casseroles, quiches, and cold vegetable salads.

But you had better hurry if you want to try it. I'm sorry to say, but, like farmland, the wild foods once so much a part of life in the rural South have begun to vanish. It may not be too many more years before the only greens I can harvest in the spring will be those I plant in my kitchen garden. Gone, too, will be summer's wild buckberries, yellow plums, and sweet mulberries; the wild muscadines and sugar berries of the fall; and the hickory nuts we gather in the winter. It will be sad if that happens, but we will go on and make do, just as we always have.

THE RECIPES

Poke Pie
Wilted Dandelion Salad with Maple-Mustard Dressing
Mess o' Greens Salad with Warm Pecan Dressing
Country-Style Turnip Greens
Spring Harvest Salad

Wild Weed Flowers

You will not find fancy, decorative foods and garnishes in my house. A pretty bowl filled with steaming-hot fresh vegetables, a platter of crisp, golden-brown fried chicken, baskets piled high with freshly baked muffins and breads, and a fresh cake under a glass dome offer unsurpassed beauty in their pure simplicity.

But flowers are never absent from my house. Everywhere are delicate bunches and sprigs of wildflowers in "vases" made of blue Vicks jars, amber cough syrup bottles, and brown glass Clorox jugs.

I find it hard not to love the wild weed flowers like the morning glory. Even knowing that the dreaded field bindweed, also commonly known as cardinal climber, moonflower, creeping charley, or cornbind, could, if not arrested, wipe out our fields of corn, I am still in awe of its compelling beauty.

So I admit that I let a few survive near my house, to be picked in the early morning hours and floated in the pressed-glass, footed, fruit compote that alone survived when our original family home burned to the ground.

I also look favorably upon the blooming mean grass and the common yellow wood sorrel with its cloverlike leaf and delicate yellow buttercup-shaped flowers. These are weeds that I set out with all good intentions to kill. But when they are gathered and arranged with wild wheat, yellow nutsedge, crimson clover, and Queen Anne's lace, they offer a beautiful addition to the table. No, flowers—whether they're weeds or not—will never be absent from my house.

POKE PIE

Serves 6 to 8

The water you drain off when boiling poke is usually red. Some cooks suggest boiling the poke a second time, after which the water will be relatively clear, but I think that one boiling is enough—otherwise you lose too much of the flavor. Also, be sure to cook poke leaves whole to maintain their vitamin content, chopping them only after blanching.

**Enough poke salad sprouts (very young pokeweed) to yield 3 cups
of blanched poke (about 2 ½ pounds uncooked)
2 tablespoons olive oil
3 cloves garlic, minced or grated
½ teaspoon minced fresh basil
½ teaspoon minced fresh sage
½ cup all-purpose flour
½ cup cornmeal
½ teaspoon salt
3 eggs, lightly beaten
¼ cup freshly grated Parmesan cheese**

1. Pull the leaves from the pokeweed, discard the stems, and rinse the leaves well. Bring a large kettle of water to a boil. Add the pokeweed leaves and boil for 3 to 4 minutes. Drain in a colander and discard the water. Chop the poke roughly and set aside.

2. Preheat oven to 400° F. In a large cast-iron skillet, heat the olive oil over medium-low heat until the oil begins to jump a bit. Add the garlic, basil, and sage and saute, stirring occasionally, for 2 minutes. Add the blanched poke sprouts, stir to combine, and remove from heat.

3. In a small bowl, blend the flour, cornmeal, and salt and sprinkle over the poke sprouts in the skillet. Pour the beaten eggs over the top and mix well. Sprinkle with the Parmesan cheese.

4. Cover the skillet and bake in the preheated oven for 50 minutes. Remove the cover and bake for 10 to 15 minutes longer or until nicely browned. Remove from oven, cut into slices, and serve.

WILTED DANDELION SALAD WITH MAPLE-MUSTARD DRESSING

Serves 2

When gathering wild dandelions, make sure you pick only from lawns or meadows that are totally free from herbicides and pesticides. If pepper-seasoned bacon is not available in your area, make your own: take some thick-sliced bacon, rub it well on both sides with freshly ground black pepper, and let it stand in the refrigerator overnight.

5 cups torn dandelion greens (about 1 pound)
3 or 4 strips pepper-seasoned bacon
2 tablespoons strawberry vinegar or red wine vinegar
1 ½ tablespoons maple syrup
1 tablespoon Dijon mustard
1 clove garlic, crushed

1. Rinse the greens well and discard the stems. Drain leaves well and place in a large bowl.

2. In a medium skillet, cook the bacon over medium-high heat until brown and crispy, about 6 minutes. Drain on paper towels, reserving 2 teaspoons of the pan drippings in the skillet. When bacon has drained, crumble it into small pieces.

3. In a small bowl, combine the vinegar, maple syrup, mustard, and garlic and mix well. Pour this mixture into the skillet with the reserved bacon drippings and cook over medium-high heat, stirring constantly, for 2 minutes.

4. Quickly pour the dressing over the greens, add the crumbled bacon, toss to mix, and serve immediately.

MESS O' GREENS SALAD
WITH WARM PECAN DRESSING
Serves 2

The vinegar and pecan dressing for this simple salad makes it an appealing side dish, both attractive and a little bit different from what you might be used to.

6 cups fresh mustard, turnip, and/or collard greens (about 1 pound)
2 tablespoons balsamic vinegar
2 teaspoons honey
1 tablespoon Dijon mustard
2 teaspoons vegetable oil
⅓ cup pecans, roughly chopped or broken

1. Wash greens well, dry thoroughly, then remove and discard the long stems. Tear the greens into salad-size pieces and place in a large bowl.

2. In a small bowl, combine the vinegar, honey, and mustard. Set aside.

3. Heat the oil in a small skillet until hot but not smoking. Add the vinegar mixture and pecans and cook, stirring regularly, for 2 to 3 minutes. Pour over the greens and serve at once.

COUNTRY-STYLE TURNIP GREENS
Serves 6

Be sure to serve cornbread and the "pot likker" with this Southern favorite. You can substitute collards for the turnip greens if you want.

2 slices bacon
1 onion, chopped
5 to 6 pounds fresh turnip greens
1 ½ cups water
2 teaspoons sugar
½ teaspoon salt

1. In a heavy skillet, cook the bacon over medium-high heat until crisp, about 6 minutes. Remove from heat and drain well on paper towels. Remove all but 1 tablespoon of fat from the skillet. Add the onion to the skillet and cook, stirring occasionally, until tender, about 5 minutes. Remove from heat and set aside.

2. Wash turnip greens thoroughly, dry well, and remove stems. Tear greens into salad-size pieces and place in a large pot along with the

water, sugar, and salt. Bring to a boil over high heat, reduce heat to low, and simmer until tender, about 15 to 20 minutes.

3. Break the bacon into pieces. Remove the greens from the heat, stir in the bacon and onions, and serve at once.

SPRING HARVEST SALAD
Serves 4 to 6

I n our family, we all have our own kitchen gardens. We're still just as competitive as when we were kids, so there is still a race to be the first to harvest. In fact, it seems that the older we get the more intense the competition is. I do believe we are racing against time.

Late last spring during the daily check in my garden, I discovered that finally there were two beets large enough to cook. I headed for the kitchen with, can you believe, two beets totaling not quite half a pound. But dandelion greens were at their peak for picking, spring onions stood ready to be pulled, parsley and cilantro were peeking up from the ground, and there was a sparse picking of broccoli. So before long I had the first salad of spring ready for my family.

½ pound fresh beets
2 cups small fresh broccoli spears
4 cups torn young dandelion greens, washed and dried
2 green onions, finely chopped
1 large clove garlic, minced
1 tablespoon chopped fresh parsley
1 tablespoon chopped fresh cilantro
2 tablespoons chopped boiled green peanuts (optional)
3 tablespoons olive oil
2 teaspoons red wine vinegar
2 teaspoons balsamic vinegar
2 teaspoons honey
⅛ teaspoon salt, or to taste
⅛ teaspoon freshly ground black pepper, or to taste

1. In a medium saucepan, cook the beets in 1 quart boiling water until just tender, about 15 to 20 minutes. Drain, allow to cool, then peel and dice. Set aside.

2. Rinse the saucepan and bring a second quart of water to a boil over high heat. Add the broccoli spears and cook until tender and bright green, about 3 minutes. Drain and place in a bowl of ice water to chill. When chilled, drain and set aside.

3. In a large bowl, combine the beets, broccoli, dandelion greens, green onions, garlic, parsley, cilantro, and, if desired, the peanuts.

4. In a small bowl, whisk together the olive oil, vinegars, honey, and salt and pepper. Pour this vinaigrette over the vegetables and gently toss to lightly coat all ingredients. Serve immediately.

Dori's Forbidden Fruits

Some folks claim they have been able to identify correctly the wild mushrooms in our area known as morels. Maybe I have seen them as well—I have noticed mushrooms with almost sponge-like, pitted conical or rounded heads appearing in the spring along the banks of streams, at the edge of forests full of oak trees, and in the shady, cool pastures and apple orchards. But I do not pick or eat wild mushrooms. I'm not certain I would be able to avoid other, poisonous mushrooms. Nor do I eat the fungus called corn smut, which is an expensive delicacy in gourmet stores, and we grow corn with ears sometimes smothered in it. It just doesn't strike my fancy. For the same reason, I don't pick wild asparagus either. And I don't know which month pokeweed berries are safe to pick, so I don't make pokeberry jelly. Other than that, there's not much in the fields and forests of York County, South Carolina, that I will not gather and cook, as long as it's edible.

92

CHAPTER 8

The Farm Stand Recipe Swap

On any farm there is inevitably either an overabundance of fruits and vegetables or scarcely any at all. It was the overabundance of okra one summer that really got our farm stand recipe swap board going.

I had been giving recipes to my customers for some time. "Have you ever made corncob jelly?" they would ask, or some such. And I'd say, "Why, yes, my mama made it all the time. I have a recipe for it, but I don't have it on me right now. I'll bring it by here. Why don't you bring me a recipe to swap for it?"

Our peach shed, which serves as the farm stand, is easily accessible — you can just drive right up to it — so people who came by after the shed was closed for the day would tuck their recipes under a little rock. The next morning I would get to the peach shed and find recipes for the most interesting things. Sometimes the recipes would be all water-soaked if it had rained during the night, but usually I could still read them.

In the beginning, I used to put the recipes in a basket or a box at the farm stand, but, with my wonderful brothers Orestus and Jarvis helping out, the recipes always seemed to end up in the trash. So I decided to copy Orestus's example and put up a piece of cardboard like the one he uses to post the date he's going to start picking certain varieties of peaches. On my board I would post recipes. I would bring my recipes in the morning and during the day I would sit and make copies of them by hand and put them up on the board so that if people wanted one, they could just take it, free.

I discovered that some of my customers didn't buy certain things because they didn't really know how to cook them. I decided that if I had recipes for those vegetables and fruits, customers would buy more because the recipes would give them cooking ideas. For example, a customer might come by on a day when we had lots of okra and say, "Well, I don't really understand what to do with okra." Then I would say, "Oh, my, did you check the recipe board? We've got some new okra recipes over there that are very, very tasty."

Many of my new customers who had just moved to the area had never heard of green crowder peas, nor had they ever tried skillet cornbread, and they flat-out didn't like grits or okra. But over the seasons, with the patience of a fisherman, I lured them in, one by one. We have since had to increase our okra and crowder pea plantings to keep up with the demand.

The recipe swap idea really took off when I developed a recipe for okra parmigiana. I created the recipe for a Southern woman who was, without a doubt, my best customer.

Like many of my regulars, this woman usually pulled up in her car, walked down the little path that runs past the stand, and took a seat in one of the lawn chairs we keep at the back. The chairs are right by the huge oak stump that I call my "writer's stump," because when I am trying to write and have writer's block, I go sit there and hope something comes to me.

So when she drove up one Thursday afternoon, I expected her to go sit a spell in the lawn chair. As she was pulling to a stop, I was already taking out a bag to fill with a peck of okra, because every Thursday she bought a peck for the weekend.

But that Thursday was different. "No okra today," she announced as she got out of the car. Well, believe me, that hurt, because I have to pick the okra fresh every day. I can't take leftover okra home at night and put it in the refrigerator and bring it back the next day, because the okra turns black from the change of temperature. If we have any left over at the end of the day, I always make a point of taking a little nest of it to the senior citizens, especially those who used to have farms but who now live in those little complexes down in town where they can't even have gardens. On that Thursday, though, I was bone-tired and didn't feel like making that trip.

But my regular customer was standing firm. "My family said that if I put another mess o' stewed okra on the table, or okra in any form, they were gonna put me right out of the house," she said.

My heart sank. I had counted on getting a peck of okra sold. I dropped my eyes to hide my disappointment . . . and noticed in the open newspaper on a chair a recipe for eggplant parmigiana. I looked right back up at my customer. "But have you ever served them okra parmigiana?" I asked.

She said, "Okra what? What's that?"

And I said, "Well, I don't have the recipe with me right now, but if you stop by here tomorrow, I'll have it."

She promised to come back the next day. So I stopped at the grocery store after we closed the peach shed that evening, bought the ingredients for eggplant parmigiana, and spent most of the night creating a recipe for okra parmigiana.

When the peach shed opened the next morning, filled with freshly picked okra, the recipe was ready. I made copies of it and put them up on the swap board, and that's all it took. People saw the recipe and wanted to try it, so they bought okra. In fact, that recipe proved so popular that it spawned other similar recipes: fried green tomato parmigiana, vegetarian okra lasagna, a salad of okra, tomatoes, and corn—the list goes on and on.

My customers now come from miles away not just to buy my produce but also to get recipes from the board and to tack up their own. So many wonderful recipes have been posted that it was very hard to pick and choose among them, but I have done my best and selected a few for you to try.

THE RECIPES

Okra Parmigiana
Southern Vegetable Lasagna
Summer Cabbage with Sweet Potatoes and Okra
Fried Green Tomato Parmigiana
Stuffed Roly-Poly Zucchini
Summer Fruit Salad with Peach Dressing
Cantaloupe Mousse
"Tastes Like Apple" Zucchini Pie

OKRA PARMIGIANA
Serves 6

I may not be a *mama Italiana*, but I am a Southerner, and I want taste in my tomato sauce, too, so I make my own. I use home-canned tomatoes, but store-bought canned tomatoes are fine as well. Be sure to get whole tomatoes, though, so you can chop them in big pieces and get a nice, chunky sauce. Make sure you use fresh-picked okra, too. Served with a hearty salad and hot garlic bread, this delicious dish makes a satisfying summer meal.

About 4 tablespoons olive oil
¾ cup chopped onions
¾ cup chopped celery
¼ cup chopped fresh parsley
2 cloves garlic, minced
One 14-ounce can whole tomatoes, undrained, roughly chopped
One 6-ounce can tomato paste
Salt and freshly ground black pepper to taste
1 pound fresh okra pods, each about 3 inches long, washed
2 eggs, lightly beaten
1 cup seasoned bread crumbs
½ cup freshly grated Parmesan cheese

1. Preheat oven to 350° F.
2. In a large, heavy skillet, heat 1 tablespoon of the olive oil over medium-high heat until hot but not smoking. Add the onion, celery,

parsley, and garlic and cook, stirring occasionally, until tender, about 5 to 7 minutes.

3. Stir in the tomatoes and tomato paste and season to taste with salt and pepper. Reduce heat to low, cover, and simmer for 45 minutes, stirring occasionally.

4. Remove the caps from the okra pods and slice the pods in half lengthwise. Dip into the egg and then roll in the bread crumbs to coat. Heat 2 tablespoons of the olive oil in the skillet over medium-high heat until hot but not smoking. Add a single layer of okra slices and brown on both sides, about 3 minutes per side. Remove, drain on paper towels, and set aside. Repeat with remaining okra slices, adding more oil if necessary.

5. Layer half the okra in a lightly greased 13" x 9" x 2" baking dish. Spoon half of the tomato sauce over the okra slices. Repeat the two layers. Top with Parmesan cheese and bake in the preheated oven for 45 to 50 minutes or until bubbly and browned.

SOUTHERN VEGETABLE LASAGNA
Serves 6 to 8

I now have a lot of vegetarian customers at the farm stand. They drive sparkling clean pickup trucks and those little Jeep Cherokees and they are very upper middle class, so I call them "Vuppies." They have their weekend cabins by the creek and they play lots of tennis and golf.

When they stop by my stand, I like to introduce them to all the wonderful Southern vegetables, things like crowder peas and okra and mustard greens. I had the Vuppies in mind when I created this recipe for vegetarian lasagna in which okra takes the place of sausage, mustard greens replace spinach, and sweet potatoes add their own delicious Southern flavor.

10 dried lasagna noodles (about 6 ounces)
1 ½ pounds fresh mustard greens (you can substitute spinach)
2 cups sliced fresh mushrooms
1 cup grated sweet potatoes
½ cup chopped onion
½ cup fresh okra, caps removed and pods thinly sliced
1 tablespoon olive oil
2 cups tomato sauce, freshly made or canned
One 6-ounce can tomato paste
1 tablespoon finely chopped fresh oregano
2 cups small-curd cottage cheese, drained
1 pound mozzarella or Monterey Jack cheese, thinly sliced
¼ cup freshly grated Parmesan cheese

1. Preheat oven to 375° F.

2. In a large saucepan, bring 5 quarts of unsalted water to a rapid boil over high heat. Add the lasagna noodles slowly, 2 or 3 at a time. Cook until tender, 8 to 10 minutes, and drain.

3. Wash the greens well, tear into medium-size pieces, and place in a medium saucepan over medium-high heat. Using only the water that clings from the washing, cook for 4 to 5 minutes, turning occasionally, until well wilted. Remove from pan and set aside.

4. In a medium bowl, combine the mushrooms, sweet potato, onion, and okra. In a medium saucepan, heat the olive oil over medium-high heat until hot but not smoking. Add the vegetables and cook, stirring frequently, for 6 to 8 minutes or until tender but not browned. Add the tomato sauce, tomato paste, oregano, and wilted greens, stir to combine, and heat through. Set aside.

5. Layer half the lasagna noodles in a well-greased 13" x 9" x 2" baking dish. Cover with half the cottage cheese, half the tomato-vegetable mixture, and half the mozzarella or Monterey Jack. Repeat the four layers.

6. Bake in the preheated oven for 30 to 35 minutes or until the mixture is bubbly and the top is lightly browned. Let stand for 10 to 12 minutes before serving. Serve with a dish of freshly grated Parmesan cheese for sprinkling.

SUMMER CABBAGE WITH SWEET POTATOES AND OKRA
Serves 6

This recipe is so good that my sister Virginia will even serve it to company on Sundays, and cabbage is not a food we Southerners generally serve to guests. When you make this dish, try to get hold of a cabbage that has just been cut from the stalk—what we call a "new" cabbage. It will taste quite different from a cabbage that has been refrigerated, because as soon as cabbages are chilled they begin to lose their flavor.

1 medium head new cabbage (about 2 pounds), washed and dried
2 tablespoons garlic oil (page 170), or grease from 2 strips bacon
1 medium sweet potato, peeled and sliced into very thin strips with
a vegetable peeler (as you would a carrot)
½ pound small fresh okra, stems cut off but caps left on
1 tablespoon white distilled vinegar
Salt and pepper to taste

1. Trim away the outside leaves of the cabbage, cut it in quarters, and cut away most of the core, leaving just enough to hold the leaves together. Cut the leaves into thin strips, rinse well in a colander, and set aside to drain.

2. In a medium skillet, heat the oil over medium-high heat. Add the cabbage leaves and cook for 3 to 4 minutes or until the cabbage is slightly wilted, using only the water clinging to the leaves from their washing.

3. Add the sweet potato and okra and stir lightly to mix. Sprinkle with the vinegar and salt and pepper. Cover with a close-fitting lid and continue to cook, gently stirring occasionally, for 12 to 15 minutes or until tender. Serve hot.

FRIED GREEN TOMATO PARMIGIANA

Serves 6

My sister Virginia created this recipe as a new way to use the fried green tomatoes that are so popular in our part of the country. I suspect that she decided to create it because she wanted an excuse not to help out at the farm stand one hot summer day. This recipe is a bit different from my okra parmigiana, but I must admit, it's almost as good.

4 medium green tomatoes, cut into ½-inch slices
⅛ teaspoon salt, or to taste
⅛ teaspoon sugar
2 egg whites
¾ cup seasoned bread crumbs
2 ½ tablespoons olive oil
1 cup chopped onions
3 large cloves garlic, finely chopped
2 cups tomato sauce, freshly made or canned
One 6-ounce can tomato paste
1 tablespoon each, fresh and finely chopped: basil, parsley, sage
Salt and freshly ground black pepper to taste
2 cups grated Muenster or mozzarella cheese
2 teaspoons finely chopped fresh oregano
½ cup freshly grated Parmesan cheese

1. Preheat oven to 350° F.

2. Place the tomato slices in a colander, sprinkle with the salt and sugar, and set aside in the sink.

3. In a small bowl, beat the egg whites until peaks form. Dip the tomato slices one at a time into the egg whites, coat with the bread crumbs, and place on a lightly oiled baking sheet.

4. In a large, heavy skillet, heat 1 ½ tablespoons of the olive oil over medium heat until hot but not smoking. Add a single layer of tomatoes and brown on both sides, about 3 minutes per side. Drain on paper towels and set aside. Repeat with remaining slices.

5. Using the same skillet, heat 1 tablespoon of olive oil over medium heat until hot but not smoking. Add the onion and garlic and cook, stirring occasionally, until tender, about 5 to 7 minutes. Add the tomato sauce, tomato paste, basil, parsley, and sage. Season to taste with salt and pepper and continue to cook, stirring occasionally, for 10 to 12 minutes.

6. Layer half the green tomatoes in a lightly greased 13" x 9" x 2" baking dish. Spoon half of the sauce and sprinkle half of the Muenster or mozzarella cheese over the tomato slices. Repeat the layers, reserving a little sauce for the top layer.

7. In a small bowl, mix the oregano and Parmesan cheese. Sprinkle evenly over the top layer of sauce and bake in the preheated oven for 45 to 50 minutes or until the top is well browned and the tomatoes are tender. Serve hot.

STUFFED ROLY-POLY ZUCCHINI
Serves 6 to 8

I created this recipe when *Burpee's Seed Catalogue* introduced a new summer vegetable, roly-poly zucchini. Almost every cook tried to create her own recipe using the new vegetable, and here's mine. Any type of zucchini or summer squash can be substituted here.

4 medium roly-poly zucchini
½ cup grated Swiss cheese
½ cup sour cream
½ cup finely chopped cooked country ham (page 36)
⅓ cup freshly grated Parmesan cheese
2 large eggs
¼ teaspoon salt, or to taste
¼ teaspoon freshly ground black pepper, or to taste

1. Preheat the oven to 400° F.

2. In a large saucepan, bring about 3 inches of water to a boil over high heat. Add the zucchini whole and boil for 5 minutes. Drain and place immediately in cold water to cool. When cool, slice each zucchini in half lengthwise and, using a melon baller, scoop out the center, leaving a ⅛-inch-thick shell. Place the zucchini shells, cut side up, in a single layer in a shallow baking pan.

3. Coarsely chop the scooped-out zucchini and drain well in a colander. When drained, combine the chopped zucchini with the Swiss cheese, sour cream, ham, and Parmesan cheese in a small bowl. Stir in the eggs, salt, and pepper and mix well. Fill the zucchini shells with this mixture.

4. Bake in the preheated oven for 35 to 40 minutes or until the top is nicely browned. Serve at once.

Green Peanuts

Freshly dug peanuts are not hard in the hand, but tender and soft. Right after the plants are dug, they are stacked to dry on racks up off the ground in the sun. Or you can hang them in your shed or loft or even in an empty room. After a month or six weeks, they will be thoroughly dried out. Then the peanuts will be as most people know them, hard and crunchy. But when they are freshly dug, they are soft and chewy, even after they are boiled or baked. It is at this stage that peanuts taste almost exactly like those very expensive pine nuts sold in gourmet stores.

SUMMER FRUIT SALAD
WITH PEACH DRESSING
Serves 4 to 6

Yes, kiwi does grow in South Carolina, and this is a great way to use it.

2 medium fresh peaches, sliced
2 bananas, sliced
1 tablespoon fresh lemon juice
½ head lettuce, chopped
2 cups cubed fresh pineapple (you can substitute canned)
2 kiwis, peeled and sliced

1. Place the peaches and bananas in a large bowl, sprinkle with the lemon juice, and mix gently.

2. Line a large plate with the chopped lettuce, arrange the peaches, bananas, pineapple, and kiwi on top, and drizzle lightly with peach dressing. Serve immediately, along with the remaining peach dressing in a small bowl or pitcher.

PEACH DRESSING
Makes about 1½ cups

2 medium fresh peaches, peeled and pitted
¼ cup vegetable oil
2 tablespoons fresh orange juice
2 tablespoons flaked coconut (optional)
1 ½ teaspoons fresh lime juice
1 teaspoon grated nutmeg

Combine all the ingredients in a food processor or blender. Process until smooth. Cover and refrigerate until well chilled.

CANTALOUPE MOUSSE
Serves 4

On summer weekends, shoppers from miles away come to my farm stand. Among the early arrivals are young women in fancy cars and minivans, a little tired from jogging, horseback riding, or a morning game of tennis.

One day I helped one of these young women—who had not a speck of a Southern accent—to select freshly pulled melons. After much discussion, she bought one large and two medium cantaloupes, telling me that she was going to use them for a "melon mousse." I was doubtful, but she made a believer out of me when she returned with the recipe.

It does indeed make a cooling and delicious dessert for a summer afternoon.

½ **large or 1 small ripe, sweet cantaloupe,**
seeded and rind removed
The juice of ½ lemon
2 teaspoons chopped fresh mint
A pinch of salt
½ teaspoon unflavored gelatin
¾ cup heavy cream
2 small cantaloupes, halved, seeded, and chilled
Fresh mint sprigs for garnish

1. In a food processor or blender, puree the peeled and seeded cantaloupe until smooth. Measure 1 cup of the puree into a small bowl, add the lemon juice, chopped mint, and salt, and mix well. Allow to stand at room temperature for 1 to 3 hours, then press through a fine sieve using the back of a wooden spoon.

2. Transfer the strained puree to a small saucepan. Sprinkle with the gelatin and allow to stand 2 to 3 minutes. Place the saucepan over low heat and stir until the gelatin is fully dissolved. Pour into a medium bowl and refrigerate until cooled and just slightly thickened, about 12 to 15 minutes.

3. In a small, chilled bowl, beat the cream until stiff peaks form. Fold a fourth of the whipped cream into the melon puree. Gently fold in the remaining whipped cream. Cover and refrigerate for at least 2 hours, gently folding once or twice during this time.

4. Mound the mousse in the chilled melon halves, garnish with mint sprigs, and serve.

Hidden Gardens

In South Carolina, slave houses were customarily built smack-dab in the middle of the cotton fields. I do believe the plantation owners put the slave houses there because they wanted the slaves where they could work all the time. Some plantation owners wouldn't allow slaves even to have gardens—they didn't want slaves wasting time or valuable land on private gardens. They wanted them out working in those cotton fields.

According to our handed-down tradition, many slave women would say to the plantation overseer, "Oh, I just want me a few buckets of hollyhocks, a few little rows of flowers." Well, the overseer couldn't find an excuse to deny a woman her little flowers, which required almost no care, so he'd give her permission. The slave women would plant their flowers, and behind the tall holly-hocks, they would hide a kitchen garden. From those gardens came the spring onions and sweet potatoes and tasty herbs and all the good, fresh vegetables that are such a part of our cooking heritage.

"TASTES LIKE APPLE" ZUCCHINI PIE

Makes one 9-inch pie

This is one of those recipes that I found folded up and tucked under a rock at the farm stand one morning. It's another sneaky way to use zucchini, which seems to multiply so rapidly in the garden. For this recipe, you must use zucchini that is large enough to have some flavor but still tender enough so you can easily stick your thumbnail through the skin. When you serve this pie, I'll bet nobody will be able to tell it's not apple.

2 or 3 medium zucchini
2 cups water
2 tablespoons fresh lemon juice
⅛ teaspoon salt, or to taste
1 ¾ cups sugar
2 teaspoons ground cinnamon
¼ teaspoon allspice
¼ teaspoon ground nutmeg
2 teaspoons cream of tartar
2 tablespoons all-purpose flour
2 tablespoons cornstarch
¼ cup chilled butter, cut into small pieces
1 unbaked 9-inch pie shell and 1 unbaked 9-inch top crust
(page 81)

1. Preheat the oven to 400° F.

2. Peel the zucchini and cut in half lengthwise. Cut each half in half lengthwise again, then remove the seeds and cut crosswise into slices about ¼ inch thick. Cut enough zucchini to total 6 cups sliced.

3. In a medium saucepan, bring the water to a boil over high heat. Add the zucchini, reduce the heat to medium-high, and cook until tender but still crisp, about 3 to 4 minutes. Drain in a colander.

4. In a medium bowl, toss together the drained zucchini, lemon juice, and salt. Set aside.

5. In a small bowl, combine the sugar, cinnamon, allspice, nutmeg, cream of tartar, flour, and cornstarch and mix well. Add to the zucchini and mix well. The mixture will be rather runny and loose.

6. Spoon the mixture into the unbaked pie shell and dot with half the butter pieces. Add the top crust, pinch together the edges to seal, and dot the crust with the remaining butter pieces. Bake in the preheated oven for 40 to 45 minutes or until golden-brown. Cool on a wire rack and serve warm or at room temperature.

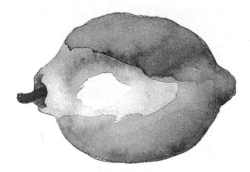

CHAPTER 9

Wild Honey in Springtime

It has been a long, long time since I noticed a swarm of bees on the move in this part of the country. But years ago it was a common sight, especially in the spring. We would hear them coming from far away. Buzzing sounds filled the air, and pretty soon you saw it—a dark cloud of bees flying through the air, nearly always followed by children throwing sand and dirt up in the air, banging on tin cans, pots, and pans, hoping to get that old queen bee to settle on *their* farm.

And you know something? For some strange reason it seemed to work. The bees would choose a tree branch or some part of a nearby structure—usually an overhang on a house or abandoned barn—and settle in a cluster. There they would hang together, cone shaped and suspended in the air, until our local beekeeper arrived to lure them into a beehive.

The beehives were simple wooden frames with honey and pollen left in them from the previous year to provide the bees with plenty of sustenance during the spring breeding season. In warm weather, bees are more active and consume more honey than in cold weather.

The following year, during May or early June, when there was plenty of honey in the hives, we would rob the bees and set to making honey candy, dividing it up to pull by hand. We'd also slip into the kitchen and sneak a little "flavor," as we called extracts, to make chewing gum out of the beeswax. At dinner there would be new spring greens to celebrate the season and warm honey gingerbread made with fresh honey right out of the comb.

Whenever I pass the few remaining wood-frame beehives on our family farm, I pause and thank the busy little honeybees who live there. I don't want to think what our world would be like if they vanished and we were suddenly without them. Such a big part of the human diet depends on insect-pollinated fruits and vegetables, and a staggering 80 percent of that pollination is done by honeybees. Bees are so essential that swarms of them are sometimes rented by owners of fruit orchards. Fortunately, peach orchards are not totally dependent on bees for pollination, so we have one less concern on our farm. Still, it's a joy to watch honeybees on the job in our orchards, transferring pollen from one peach blossom to another, faithfully practicing their seemingly simple art. It's a joy, too, to eat the peach blossom honey that is the fruit of their labor.

THE RECIPES

Skillet Wild Greens with Green Onions
Warm Honey Gingerbread
Old-Fashioned Honey Candy
Flavored Beeswax Chewing Gum

SKILLET WILD GREENS WITH GREEN ONIONS
Serves 6

This dish is a traditional spring meal when served with hard-boiled eggs and hot cornbread squares laced with fresh butter and honey. The water left on the greens after rinsing them is enough for steaming, which is the way I like them. But if you like a less tangy flavor from your greens, cover them with boiling water and simmer over low heat for five minutes instead of steaming them. Be sure to drain them well before you continue preparing the dish.

2 pounds wild field cress (creasie greens), rinsed and stemmed
2 pounds dandelion or poke greens, rinsed and stemmed
3 tablespoons butter
20 green onions, rinsed and cut into ½-inch slices
(including green part)
Salt and freshly ground black pepper to taste

1. Place the field cress and dandelion or poke greens into a large, heavy skillet over medium-high heat, cover, and cook until wilted, 3 to 5 minutes. Remove greens from skillet and set aside.

2. In the same skillet, melt the butter over medium heat, add the green onions, cover, and cook for 5 minutes, stirring once or twice.

3. Add the wilted greens to the skillet and mix thoroughly with the butter and onions. Season to taste with salt and pepper, cover, and continue to cook over moderate heat for 15 to 20 minutes or until the greens are very tender. Serve immediately.

Children's Gardens

Children love to garden, so encourage them. I believe I had my own little garden as soon as I was big enough to hold a hoe.

Vegetables that are easy to grow and quick to bear are best for youngsters. Onions, radishes, carrots, string beans, zucchini, yellow squash, and cucumbers are all good choices. Carrot seeds are very tiny, so let children mix the seeds with some clean sand for easier planting. They might as well put in some radish seeds, too. Unlike carrots, radishes come up very quickly and are ready to harvest in less than a month.

Save some radish seeds for planting near beans to help keep bean beetles away, and remember to plant marigolds to keep all kinds of insects out of the garden. Children will love learning about natural ways to keep pests away from their vegetables.

If there is enough space, let the children plant a couple of hills of pumpkins. Names or messages written with a large nail on green pumpkins in late summer will still be visible at harvesttime in the fall, when the pumpkins have turned orange and grown large.

When the vegetables are ready, let the children pick them for a family meal and earn their place at the table. They will feel very adult and you will have taught them a lot about what goes into raising food for the meals they eat every day.

WARM HONEY GINGERBREAD
Makes about a dozen squares

This recipe is so delicious that you will feel like making it even on a beautiful spring day. Just be sure to beat the eggs until they are almost as thick as whipped cream before you add them to the rest of the batter. That gives this gingerbread its wonderful texture.

2 cups all-purpose flour
¼ teaspoon baking soda
1 ½ teaspoons baking powder
½ teaspoon salt, or to taste
1 teaspoon ground ginger
1 teaspoon ground cinnamon
½ teaspoon ground cloves
⅛ teaspoon ground nutmeg
½ cup butter
½ cup light or dark brown sugar
2 large eggs
¾ cup honey
½ cup boiling water

1. Preheat oven to 350° F. In a small bowl, sift together the flour, baking soda, baking powder, salt, ginger, cinnamon, cloves, and nutmeg. Set aside.

2. In a large bowl, cream the butter until light and lemon colored. Add the brown sugar gradually, beating after each addition until light and fluffy.

3. In a separate bowl, beat the eggs until almost the texture of whipped cream. Add the eggs to the butter-sugar mixture in three parts, beating after each addition until well blended. Add a fourth of the dry ingredients and beat until well blended. Add the honey and beat until smooth. Beat in the remaining dry ingredients, add the boiling water, and stir until well blended.

4. Pour the batter into a greased 13" x 9" baking pan. Bake in the preheated oven for 25 to 30 minutes or until a knife inserted in the center comes out clean. Cut into 12 squares. Serve warm.

OLD-FASHIONED HONEY CANDY

Makes about 4 dozen ½-inch candies

It was always a special treat when this candy was divided among the children for pulling. If you want to make the most authentic version, use Watkins Strawberry Extract, a flavoring that was peddled from farm to farm in rural areas of South Carolina. You can find it in most grocery stores these days. And remember, we are talking about home-made candy here, so don't worry about forming perfect shapes.

2 cups honey
1 cup heavy cream
1 cup sugar
½ teaspoon lemon or other flavor extract

1. In a medium saucepan, combine all the ingredients and mix well. Bring the mixture to a boil over high heat. Reduce heat to medium and simmer, stirring constantly, until it reaches the hard-crack stage: when a bit of the mixture is dropped into ice water, it should separate into threads that are hard and brittle. On a candy thermometer, this stage is between 300° and 320° F.

2. Pour the mixture onto a buttered platter to cool. As soon as it is cool enough to handle (do not allow to reach room temperature), divide the mixture into several balls and pull each ball with your hands, stretching it out and reforming it and stretching it again until it holds a consistent shape and is golden in color. Form each portion into a thin log, cut into ½-inch pieces, and wrap in waxed-paper squares.

FLAVORED BEESWAX CHEWING GUM

I still enjoy one of my favorite honey treats from childhood—flavored beeswax chewing gum. Even now I can remember all the trouble we got into when we used up all Mama's "flavor." If we wanted to make chewing gum, we had to sneak the flavor—lemon extract, usually—out of the kitchen, because Mama did not buy that lemon extract to flavor beeswax. She bought it for pies and other baked goods, not for chewing gum.

2 squares fresh honeycomb, each about 2" x 2"
1 or 2 drops lemon extract
1 or 2 drops strawberry extract

Drain as much honey as possible from one square of honeycomb. Mix 1 teaspoon of the honey with 2 teaspoons water and the lemon extract. Sprinkle this mixture over the drained square of honeycomb. Repeat this procedure with the second honeycomb square, using the strawberry extract in place of the lemon. Allow to stand for 2 to 3 minutes, then pull off a piece and chew. The honeycomb will dissolve slowly as you chew and become waxier in consistency.

Picking Spring Berries

In the spring, I am often out in the fields and orchards as soon as the dawn's light begins to part the early morning fog. Sometimes in the distance I hear excited conversation punctuated by laughter and the clanging of tin buckets. It's an occasion I know well—the wild blackberry pickers, wearing long-sleeved shirts and high boots, are ready to venture into chigger-infested thickets dense with wild undergrowth. They will bravely move from one blackberry bramble full of pain-inflicting briars to another in search of bigger, riper fruit.

Competition among the pickers is intense, for at the end of the hunt the buckets will be measured and a winner declared. Then, with blue lips and full stomachs, the pickers will head for home. The gathered berries will be picked over for canning, jellies, and jams, and a few quarts will be skimmed off for fresh cobbler, pies, and breakfast syrup.

Sometimes I'm a little saddened that I'm too busy with my chores to join the pickers, but I remain ever hopeful they will share with me. No need to worry. They'll share. Farmers and farm families always have. Still do.

CHAPTER 10

The Big Eat

As a little girl, a very big day for me was when I finally mastered the art of ringing the big iron dinner bell mounted outside the house. The pull and release on its dangling rope had to be exact—just so—in order for the bell to ring loud its "ding, dong, ding, dong." I do believe that accomplishment brought me one of my greatest joys—I was allowed to summon the field-workers home for the noonday meal.

This midday feast was part of what hired hands received for a good day's work in the steamy peach orchards. Truth be told, it was cooked more for word-of-mouth praise throughout the farming community than for the pleasure of the field-workers. For the farmer, a good meal promised another reward—we were always sure of getting the same help back year after year.

In the late morning, long plank tables were set up on our back porch or under the sprawling oak trees in the wide yard. Bleached flour sacks, sewn together and crisply ironed, served as tablecloths. The tables groaned under platters of fried chicken and smothered chicken, bowls of stewed beef in onion gravy, farm-style macaroni and cheese, country ham and redeye gravy, crowder peas with snaps, and mounds of farm-fresh sliced tomatoes and sweet onions. Small galvanized tin tubs were used for the gallons of sweet lemonade our large family and the hired hands downed.

Best of all, though, I loved the breads and desserts. Hot biscuits, corn-bread squares, and rolls made from freshly dug sweet potatoes accompanied the meal, followed by juicy blackberry cobbler and warm, gooey biscuit pie.

These days, we no longer offer a noonday meal for the peach pickers. We don't have as many peaches to pick and there is no one at home anymore to cook. My sister-in-law Willie and my sister Virginia work at the peach shed while my brothers and I work alongside the pickers in the orchards.

But at the end of the summer harvest, we still commemorate the farm-hand lunch by spreading a feast—commonly called The Big Eat—in a family member's backyard. It is true that time has changed some of the details—a television set, positioned for easy viewing from the porch, has replaced the horseshoe toss and the checkerboard. But family members still serve up the same wonderful foods, everyone eats their fill, and the feeling of good company and good times remains as strong as ever.

THE RECIPES

Smothered Chicken

Crowder Peas with Snaps

Herbed Skillet Cornbread

Sweet Potato Rolls

Pickled Melon Balls

Biscuit Pie with Sweet Cinnamon-Raisin Crust

Wild Blackberry Cobbler

SMOTHERED CHICKEN
S e r v e s   4

Some people object to the sour cream in traditionally prepared smothered chicken, so for them I have devised an alternative that uses fresh peaches instead. To make it, prepare the dish as directed through step 4 in this recipe. Then add two tablespoons of water, cover the skillet tightly, and simmer over low heat for twenty-five minutes. At that point, add a cup and a half of chopped fresh peaches, cook for another ten minutes, and then remove the cover and cook ten minutes more to crisp the skin slightly. But if sour cream is what you like, just proceed with the recipe as written.

8 pieces of chicken (legs, thighs, or breasts, with or without skin)
1 cup all-purpose flour
Salt and freshly ground black pepper to taste
¼ teaspoon garlic powder (optional)
¼ teaspoon onion powder
1 teaspoon paprika
About 1 cup vegetable oil
2 medium onions, sliced thin
¾ cup sour cream
¼ cup chicken stock
¼ cup chopped green onions (including green part)
2 tablespoons water

1. Preheat oven to 350° F.

2. Wash chicken pieces and dry well. In a clean plastic or brown paper bag, combine the flour, salt, pepper, garlic powder (if desired), onion powder, and paprika. Shake a few times to mix. Place 2 to 3 pieces of chicken in the bag, shake to coat evenly, remove, and shake off excess coating. Repeat with remaining pieces of chicken.

3. In a large ovenproof skillet, heat ¼ inch of vegetable oil over medium heat until hot but not smoking. Add the chicken pieces and brown well, about 3 minutes per side. Remove from pan and set aside.

4. Pour excess oil out of the skillet, leaving just a thin layer. Add the onions and saute, stirring occasionally, until they are translucent, about 5 to 7 minutes.

5. In a medium bowl, combine the sour cream, chicken stock, green onions, and water and mix well.

6. Place the browned chicken on top of the onions in the skillet and pour the sour cream mixture over the top. Cover lightly with foil and bake in the preheated oven for 40 to 45 minutes or until the chicken is tender and shows no trace of pink near the bone. Serve at once.

CROWDER PEAS WITH SNAPS
Serves 2

Shelled, fully ripe crowder peas are delicious all by themselves, but this summer dish gains a wonderful fresh flavor when "snaps"— tender, green, undeveloped pea pods that look like young string beans— are picked, snapped into bite-size pieces, and cooked along with the crowders.

2 cups fresh crowder peas, shelled (about 3 pounds in the hull)
½ cup snap peas, broken into ½-inch pieces
Salt and freshly ground black pepper to taste
⅛ teaspoon sugar
1 tablespoon butter or drippings from 3 strips
pepper-seasoned bacon (page 87)

Put the crowders and snaps in a heavy skillet and add enough water to cover well. Bring to a boil over high heat. Reduce heat to low, add salt, pepper, sugar, and butter or bacon drippings. Cover and simmer gently for 15 to 20 minutes or until tender. Serve at once, either as a side dish or spooned over hot skillet cornbread (below).

HERBED SKILLET CORNBREAD

Serves 6 to 8

Corn has always been especially important to the diet of many Southern farmers, particularly during the years when the dreaded boll weevil wreaked havoc on the cotton crop. There are dozens of varieties of cornbread cooked in the South: corn pone, hoecake, hush puppies, spoon bread, and for a few old-timers, crackling bread and ash cake cornbread, the last one laying claim to medicinal value. Many farmers still openly boast that they love their cornbread better than cake. This is our family's standard buttermilk cornbread recipe, but I have dressed it up with some fresh herbs, which I think provide a refreshing taste.

1 cup cornmeal
½ cup all-purpose flour
1 tablespoon sugar
1 tablespoon baking powder
½ teaspoon salt
1 cup buttermilk
¼ cup bacon drippings (you can substitute melted butter)
2 eggs, lightly beaten
1 teaspoon each, fresh and finely chopped:
chives, parsley, sage, thyme

1. Preheat oven to 400° F.

2. In a medium bowl, combine the cornmeal, flour, sugar, baking powder, and salt.

3. Add the buttermilk, bacon drippings or melted butter, and eggs and stir until just combined. Add the herbs and stir until the mixture is smooth.

4. Grease a heavy 9-inch cast-iron skillet and set in the preheated oven for about 4 minutes. Remove from oven, pour in the batter, and bake for about 20 to 25 minutes or until the top is golden-brown and a knife inserted in the center comes out clean. Cool on a wire rack, cut into large pieces, and serve warm or at room temperature.

Making Bread

My earliest memories of making bread go back to the cold, cold winter days of my childhood. Dressed in a long-sleeved red plaid flannel dress, a wool sweater, tan ribbed cotton stockings, and brown high-top, lace-up shoes, I stood on a little wooden stool in the pantry. Next to the stool were round, metal-banded wooden barrels filled with flour and cornmeal. A large floured board, placed on top of the cornmeal barrel, held a big, troughlike wooden bowl.

I remember watching my mama turn out the lump of dough from the bowl onto the smooth floured board and begin to knead. When the dough was smooth and she could pull it kind of like an elastic band, she started shaping pinched-off pieces of dough into balls. I caught on quickly when she showed me how to shape the balls, and I helped. Sometimes I was even allowed to dip the balls into the bowl of butter kept melted by repeated trips to the cookstove in the kitchen.

My mama arranged the butter-dipped balls of dough in her favorite fluted tube cake pan, covered the pan with a tea towel, and placed it in the warmer over the stove to rise. She made the leftover pieces of dough into biscuit pie or individual pan-fried butter stickies, little rounds of dough rich with butter and sugar and milk syrup. The stickies were shared among the younger siblings and eaten as soon as they had cooled enough not to burn our mouths. No wonder helping to make bread was a chore I loved.

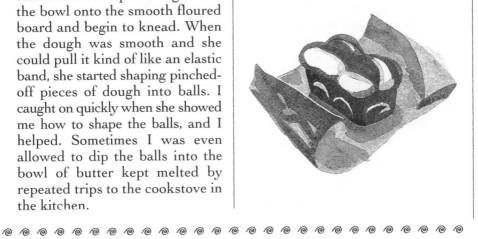

SWEET POTATO ROLLS
Makes 1½ dozen

These little rolls taste best when served hot from the oven. My sister Virginia sometimes adds one small, thinly sliced, mildly hot banana pepper to turn them into hot-pepper rolls. You can also substitute white potatoes for the sweet potatoes if you wish.

¼ cup warm water
3 tablespoons sugar
1 tablespoon active dry yeast
2 eggs
⅓ cup milk
¼ cup plus 1 tablespoon unsalted butter, melted and cooled
1 teaspoon salt
¾ cup cooked, mashed, and sieved sweet potato
(about 1 large or 2 small potatoes)
3 ½ cups all-purpose flour
2 tablespoons unsalted butter, not melted

1. In a small bowl, combine the warm water with 1 tablespoon of the sugar. Sprinkle the yeast over this mixture and allow to proof for 5 minutes or until foamy.

2. In a large bowl, whisk together the proofed yeast mixture, remaining 2 tablespoons sugar, and the eggs, milk, ¼ cup melted butter, salt, and potatoes until well combined. Stir in 3 cups of the flour, 1 cup at a time.

3. Turn the dough out onto a floured surface and knead, using some of

the remaining flour to keep it from sticking, until smooth and elastic. Shape into a ball, place in a large bowl that has been coated with the remaining 2 tablespoons of butter, and turn to coat with the butter. Cover with plastic wrap and let rise in a warm place until doubled in size, about 1 hour.

4. Preheat oven to 400° F. Cut or pinch off walnut-size pieces of dough and form into balls. Put three balls of dough into each buttered muffin-tin cup, brush the tops with the reserved tablespoon of melted butter, and allow to rise, covered loosely, in a warm place until almost double in size, 30 to 45 minutes.

5. Bake in the preheated oven until golden, about 12 to 15 minutes. Serve immediately.

PICKLED MELON BALLS
Makes about 3 pints

For this recipe I like to use the Congo watermelon, which is the one with dark green stripes. It is denser than most other varieties, so it stands up better to the pickling process. If you wish, you can substitute cantaloupe or honeydew melon. You will need about ten cups of melon balls no matter what type of melon you use.

1 whole medium Congo watermelon
2 quarts water
½ cup salt
3 lemons, sliced very thin and seeds removed
4 ½ cups sugar
2 tablespoons crystallized ginger, chopped fine

1. Cut the watermelon in half lengthwise and remove seeds. Use a melon baller to make watermelon balls. You should have about 10 cups when finished.

2. In a large container, combine the melon balls, water, and salt. Cover and soak overnight.

3. Drain the melon balls and rinse well with cold water. Place in a large, heavy pot, add the lemons, sugar, ginger, and enough water to just cover the fruit. Cook over low heat until the syrup is clear, about 20 minutes.

4. Remove the fruit with a slotted spoon and pack in hot, sterilized Ball Mason jars, leaving a ¼-inch space at the top of each jar. Continue to boil the syrup until a soft, coarse thread is formed when a bit of the syrup is dropped from a spoon into chilled water (on a candy thermometer, this stage is between 230° and 234° F), about 8 to 10 minutes. Pour the syrup over the fruit in the jars. Wipe the jars rims with a clean, damp cloth, fit them with hot lids, and tightly screw on the metal rings. Process in a bath of boiling water for 10 minutes (the water should cover the jars by about 1 inch), cool on a wire rack, and store in a cool, dark place.

BISCUIT PIE WITH SWEET CINNAMON-RAISIN CRUST
(Makes one 9-inch pie)

Using this old family recipe, you can make a delicious pie even when all you have on hand are the ingredients for bread. Be sure that the "biscuits" are tightly packed when you place them in the pie shell so that they absorb all the rich milk syrup when it's time to pour it over them.

1 ½ cups all-purpose flour
½ cup shortening
⅛ teaspoon salt
¼ cup ice water (or slightly more, as needed)
¼ pound chilled butter, cut into small pieces
2 cups sugar
1 teaspoon ground nutmeg
2 teaspoons ground cinnamon
2 cups milk
1 teaspoon vanilla extract
1 teaspoon lemon extract
1 unbaked 9-inch cinnamon-raisin pie shell (page 130)

1. Preheat oven to 350° F.

2. In a medium bowl, cut together the flour, shortening, and salt with a pastry blender until the mixture has the appearance of coarse crumbs. Add the ice water and mix until it just forms a dough.

3. On a floured surface, roll out the dough until it is the thickness of pie crust. Dot with the butter, then sprinkle with 1 cup of the sugar, along with the nutmeg and cinnamon. Roll up the dough like a jelly roll.

4. Cut the rolled dough into slices about 2 inches thick and place cut side up in the uncooked pie shell. The slices should be packed tightly so their sides touch.

5. Bake in the preheated oven for 15 to 20 minutes, until the top is nicely browned.

6. Meanwhile, in a small saucepan, combine the milk, the remaining cup of sugar, and the vanilla and lemon extracts. Cook over medium-low heat, stirring regularly, for 8 to 10 minutes. Remove from heat and pour over rounds in pie shell. Return pie to oven and continue baking for 8 to 10 minutes more. Cool slightly on a wire rack and serve warm.

SWEET CINNAMON-RAISIN PIE CRUST
Makes one 9-inch shell

For a more intense flavor, you may lightly dust this crust with additional cinnamon.

1 ½ cups all-purpose flour
2 teaspoons sugar
½ teaspoon salt
½ teaspoon ground cinnamon
½ cup chilled shortening, cut into pieces
4 to 5 tablespoons ice water
¼ cup raisins

1. In a large bowl, sift together the flour, sugar, salt, and cinnamon. Cut in the shortening with a pastry blender until the mixture forms small pea-sized balls. Sprinkle 1 tablespoon of ice water over the mixture and gently toss to blend. Repeat until all dry ingredients are lightly moistened. Stir in raisins and form into a ball.

2. Flatten the ball on a lightly floured surface. Roll from center of ball to edges until dough is about ⅛ inch thick.

3. Fit the pastry into a 9-inch pie plate, then trim it to about ½ to 1 inch beyond the edge of the plate. Fold the pastry edge under and flute it. Cover the pie shell with waxed paper and refrigerate until ready to use. Do not freeze the crust, and use within 24 hours.

WILD BLACKBERRY COBBLER
Serves 6 to 8

Summer means fresh wild blackberries. My mama always made sure we picked enough to make this unusual cobbler, which has a pie-pastry bottom as well as a biscuitlike top. If you don't have blackberries, you can substitute raspberries, blueberries, or tiny wild strawberries.

4 cups fresh blackberries
2 tablespoons cornstarch
1 tablespoon fresh lemon juice
1 teaspoon grated lemon rind
¾ cup sugar, or to taste
4 tablespoons unsalted butter, melted
¾ cup all-purpose flour
¾ teaspoon baking powder
⅛ teaspoon ground nutmeg
⅛ teaspoon salt
1 large egg
2 tablespoons light cream
1 recipe orange-crust pie pastry (page 140)

1. Preheat oven to 350° F.

2. In a medium bowl, combine the berries with the cornstarch, lemon juice, lemon rind, ½ cup of the sugar, and 2 tablespoons of the butter and stir well. Set aside.

3. In a small bowl, combine the flour, the remaining ¼ cup sugar, the baking powder, nutmeg, and salt and mix well. In a separate small bowl, combine the egg, cream, and remaining 2 tablespoons of butter and mix lightly. Combine the egg mixture with the flour mixture and mix to form a soft dough.

4. Spoon the blackberry mixture into a pie plate lined with orange-crust pastry. Drop the flour-egg mixture onto the blackberry mixture by tablespoons, covering the blackberries almost completely. Bake in the preheated oven for 40 to 45 minutes or until the topping is golden. Cool on a wire rack and serve warm or at room temperature.

CHAPTER 11

Box Suppers

An old saying I remember from way back is, "Feed a man good food and you will have him eating right out of your hand." And everybody knew that was why people in York County, South Carolina, held "box suppers." That, and the added reason that if a housewife wanted to replenish her flavor cabinet free of charge, all she had to do was let the Watkins traveling salesman know that she was holding a box supper. Watkins salesmen loved such events because that was when farm women would really buy—not only vanilla and lemon extracts, but also almond, strawberry, orange, banana, pineapple, and any other new flavorings the salesman might have, plus seasonings.

Box suppers, although attended by all the families in the area, were really a singles' event, and no extravagance was too great. It was the time when every single woman, young or old, could show off not only her good cooking but also a new dress. And there was always the hope that, in the process, she would ignite a courtship that might lead to marriage.

The procedure for box suppers was simple. Each single woman who wanted to participate— and all of them did—would prepare a box of food. Every box had to contain exactly the same

menu: four pieces of fried chicken, four biscuits or rolls, two pieces of pie, and two slices of cake.

Of course, every woman wanted to show off by making the crispiest, most tender chicken and the lightest, fluffiest rolls or biscuits. When it came to the pies and cakes, there was no telling what might be included, because dessert was where the young women really tried to outdo one another. I remember that for a long time sweet potato custard pie was the favorite because it held together so well and could be cut and packed in the box without losing its shape.

Once made, the food was packed in an unmarked shoe box tied with a ribbon and placed on a table to be auctioned off. The name of the cook was hidden, written on the bottom of the box, to be revealed only when the box had been purchased. Since the highest bidder for a box would then share the food with the cook, only single men were allowed to bid.

It was not unusual for a young girl to whisper to a young man she was trying to lure away and marry something like, "Look for mine, I'm gonna have just a little pink dot on the side of the box." Sometimes that kind of thing worked, but sometimes it didn't. The dot would be too tiny to see or on the wrong side of the box, or some such. Then, oh, there was trouble, because the highest bidder might not be the woman's choice. But everyone put on a good face and had fun with it.

So those were our box suppers. I do know that a few meaningful courtships and at least a couple of marriages resulted from them. More important, I think, was the good time everyone had. There was so little for farm women to do for fun. They didn't have the theater and they didn't have the movies. So they entertained themselves and each other through food, while at the same time trying to make a few good matches.

THE RECIPES

Buttermilk Southern Fried Chicken
Heavenly Flour-Bread Biscuits
Sweet Potato Custard Pie in Orange Crust
Chocolate Zucchini Cake
Old-Fashioned Cornbread Cake

BUTTERMILK SOUTHERN FRIED CHICKEN
Serves 6

I don't know exactly why, but a buttermilk marinade makes for a tender, moist chicken. My sister-in-law Willie declares that it somehow enhances the flavor of the chicken as well. All I know is that this is the way we've always made it. After all, it's my mama's favorite recipe.

1 frying chicken, about 2 to 3 pounds, cut up
2 cups buttermilk
1 cup all-purpose flour
2 teaspoons salt, or to taste
1 teaspoon freshly ground black pepper, or to taste
1 teaspoon paprika
¼ teaspoon garlic powder (optional)
¼ teaspoon onion powder (optional)
About ½ cup vegetable oil

1. Wash chicken pieces thoroughly and pat dry. Place chicken in a long, shallow glass baking dish. Pour the buttermilk over the chicken, cover, and refrigerate for at least 4 hours, turning once or twice.

2. In a clean plastic or brown paper bag, combine the flour, salt, pepper, paprika, and, if desired, the garlic and onion powders. Place 2 or 3 pieces of chicken in the bag and shake well to coat evenly. Repeat until all chicken has been coated with seasoned flour mixture.

3. In a large, heavy skillet, heat approximately ½ inch of oil over medium-high heat until hot but not smoking. Add chicken (in batches if necessary) and brown on all sides, about 3 minutes per side. Place browned chicken on a warm platter until all pieces are cooked.

4. When all the chicken pieces are browned, crowd them into the skillet, turn heat to medium-low, cover, and cook, turning occasionally, until tender, about 35 to 40 minutes. Remove cover, turn heat to medium-high, and cook 6 to 8 minutes more or until skin is crispy. Serve at once.

HEAVENLY FLOUR-BREAD BISCUITS
Makes about 3½ dozen

The dough for these delicious biscuits is very accommodating: it does not need to rise, so you can make it in a hurry. But if you want a lighter biscuit, you *can* let the dough rise for twenty minutes prior to baking. And if you want to plan ahead, you can make the dough the day before and store it in the refrigerator overnight. Whichever you choose, the biscuits will have a wonderful flavor. The recipe makes a big batch, but you can be sure they won't last long.

1 tablespoon active dry yeast
2 tablespoons warm water
5 cups sifted all-purpose flour
¼ cup sugar
2 teaspoons baking powder
1 teaspoon salt
1 cup shortening
2 cups buttermilk

1. In a medium bowl, dissolve the yeast in the warm water. Set aside.

2. In a large bowl, sift together the flour, sugar, baking powder, and salt. Cut in the shortening with a pastry blender until the mixture resembles very coarse cornmeal.

3. Add the buttermilk to the yeast water, stir briefly, and add to the flour mixture. Stir until the mixture is just moistened. The dough, which will be very soft, may be covered and refrigerated overnight at this point.

4. Preheat oven to 400° F. Turn the dough out onto a floured surface, sprinkle the top lightly with flour, and knead 6 to 8 times. Reflour the surface and roll the dough out to a thickness of about ¼ inch. Using a biscuit cutter lightly dipped in flour, cut into rounds and place on a lightly greased baking sheet. For lighter biscuits, cover with a towel and let rise in a warm place for 20 minutes. For quick biscuits, proceed directly to baking.

5. Bake in the preheated oven for 15 to 20 minutes or until golden. Serve warm.

Chili Peppers

In York County, South Carolina, we often use crumbled dried red chili peppers in our recipes. Of course, no woman wants to admit that she grows hot peppers, because people will say it just shows she is hot tempered. So, instead, a woman will say, "Aw, my husband planted that little ol' patch of peppers, so I use 'em"—and all the while she and her neighbors are competing with each other to see who can raise the hottest peppers!

SWEET POTATO CUSTARD PIE
IN ORANGE CRUST

M a k e s o n e 1 0 - i n c h p i e

This rich pie has a delicate flavor, and the orange-nutmeg crust goes just right with the taste of sweet potatoes. It's best when served warm because you get more flavor from the crust then.

3 large eggs, beaten
1 cup sugar
2 cups cooked, mashed, and sieved sweet potatoes
(about 2 large or 3 small sweet potatoes)
⅓ cup milk
⅓ cup light cream
¼ cup butter, melted
1 tablespoon fresh orange juice
1 teaspoon vanilla extract
⅛ teaspoon lemon extract
A large pinch of freshly grated nutmeg (optional)
1 unbaked 10-inch orange-crust pie shell (page 140)

1. Preheat oven to 350° F.

2. In a medium bowl, combine the eggs, sugar, and sweet potato and beat together to mix thoroughly. Add the milk and light cream and stir until combined. Add the melted butter, orange juice, vanilla extract, lemon extract, and nutmeg and stir to mix well.

3. Pour the mixture into the unbaked pie shell and bake in the pre-heated oven for 40 to 45 minutes or until the custard is set and a knife inserted in the middle comes out clean. Best when served warm.

ORANGE-CRUST PIE PASTRY

Makes two 10-inch pie shells

If you need only one shell, you can freeze half this flavorful pastry for later use. Firmly press the unneeded pastry into a ten-inch tin-foil or Pyrex pie plate, enclose it tightly in plastic wrap, place it in a gallon plastic freezer bag, and put it in the freezer. Defrost the pastry before using it for your next pie.

2 ½ cups all-purpose flour
½ teaspoon salt
½ cup chilled unsalted butter, cut into small pieces
½ cup chilled shortening, cut into small pieces
1 teaspoon grated orange rind
6 to 8 tablespoons chilled orange juice
2 teaspoons sugar
⅛ teaspoon finely grated nutmeg

1. In a large bowl, sift together the flour and salt. Cut in the butter, shortening, and orange rind with a pastry blender until the mixture has the texture of coarse crumbs.

2. In a small bowl, combine 6 tablespoons of the orange juice with the sugar and nutmeg. Using a fork or knife, cut the orange juice mix-

ture into the flour mixture to form a soft dough, adding additional orange juice if necessary. Do not overmix. Refrigerate for at least 1 hour.

3. Roll out half the chilled dough on a floured surface to form a crust about 10 inches in diameter. Firmly press the crust into a pie plate. Trim edges to ¾ inch and flute with fingers or crimp with a fork. Repeat with the second half of the dough. Freeze or use immediately.

CHOCOLATE ZUCCHINI CAKE

Serves 10 to 12

This cake is so rich it is almost like a torte—a small slice will do. I recommend that you not reveal what this cake contains, and please don't crack a smile when somebody says, "It's great not to eat zucchini again."

4 ounces unsweetened chocolate
4 large eggs
3 cups sugar
1 ½ cups vegetable oil
3 cups all-purpose flour
1 ½ teaspoons baking powder
1 teaspoon salt
1 teaspoon baking soda
3 cups grated fresh zucchini
1 cup chopped pecans
3 tablespoons confectioners' sugar (optional)

1. Preheat oven to 350° F.

2. In a medium saucepan, over low heat, melt the chocolate, stirring frequently to avoid burning. Set aside to cool.

3. In a large bowl, beat the eggs until thick and light colored. Add the sugar, oil, and cool, melted chocolate and mix to combine.

4. In another large bowl, combine the flour, baking powder, salt, and baking soda and mix well. Add to the wet ingredients in two batches, mixing well after each addition. Stir in the zucchini and pecans.

5. Pour the batter into a greased and floured tube pan and bake in the preheated oven for about 1 hour and 20 minutes or until the cake springs back when lightly touched and a knife inserted in the cake comes out clean. Cool cake in the pan on a wire rack for 10 minutes, then loosen edges and turn out on a rack to cool completely. Sprinkle top with confectioners' sugar, if desired, and serve.

OLD-FASHIONED CORNBREAD CAKE

Serves 8 to 10

This sturdy single-layer cake takes well to any kind of flavoring. This recipe uses lemon, but there are lots of other possibilities. You can substitute the lemon ingredients with orange ones, or you can use two tablespoons of ground almonds in place of the lemon rind and substitute one teaspoon of almond extract for both the lemon juice and lemon extract. Use whatever you have on hand—it's likely to work just fine.

1 cup yellow cornmeal, plus 1 additional
tablespoon for dusting pan
½ cup all-purpose flour
1 ½ teaspoons baking powder
¼ teaspoon salt
1 cup sugar
¼ cup vegetable oil
2 tablespoons butter, softened
2 large eggs, plus 2 egg whites
½ cup heavy cream
2 teaspoons grated lemon rind
1 tablespoon fresh lemon juice
½ teaspoon lemon extract

1. Preheat oven to 350° F. Lightly grease a round 10-inch cake pan, line the bottom with wax paper, and grease the paper well. Dust with 1 tablespoon cornmeal.

2. In a medium bowl, sift together 1 cup cornmeal and the flour, baking powder, and salt. Set aside.

3. In a large bowl, beat together the sugar, oil, and 2 tablespoons butter until well blended. Add the eggs and egg whites one at a time, gently stirring after each addition until just combined.

4. In a small bowl, stir together the cream, lemon rind, lemon juice, and lemon extract, then gently stir into the sugar-egg mixture. Stir in the cornmeal-flour mixture just until blended. Be careful not to overmix.

5. Spoon the batter into the prepared pan, smooth the top with the back of the spoon, and bake in the preheated oven for 40 to 45 minutes or until the top is golden and a knife inserted into the center of the cake comes out clean.

6. Cool for 8 to 10 minutes on a wire rack, then turn cake out onto a cake plate. Peel off the waxed paper. Serve warm or at room temperature.

CHAPTER 12

Silver Teas

I t is said that Aunt Vestula brought the tradition of silver teas to us from the Low Country of South Carolina. I don't know about that, but I do know that a silver tea was a rare treat.

This event, which was always held on a Sunday afternoon, was called a silver tea because you didn't dare go to one and eat what was served unless you brought a few silver coins with you for the hostess. It was an opportunity for farm women to get together socially and also to raise a little money.

Silver teas held at our house were always staged on the front porch. When the guests arrived, they dropped their coins—which usually totaled at least twenty-five cents—into a small, pressed-glass bowl conveniently placed near the front door.

Dressed in their Sunday best, the women arrived early. Some brought aprons along just in case extra help might be needed in the kitchen. Others brought cookies, or a churn to make ice cream. They did this not because helping meant they could share the money, but because they had brought their families along and didn't want to burden the hostess with feeding so many extra guests by herself. Only the women were expected to contribute silver and to sit on the front porch; the husbands and children, not formally invited but knowing they were also welcome and would be served as well, settled in the yard in the shade of nearby oak trees.

As the afternoon wore on, the women would sit there on the porch, sipping tea and eating ever so daintily, talking over all kinds of things. I still remember helping to serve them their tea. The cups and saucers never matched, because we had to borrow from everyone we knew to have enough, but the tea was poured from a silver teapot. I don't remember whose it was, though. Our family certainly didn't own a silver teapot. But we did share some of the best of Aunt Vestula's cooking, such as her delectable lemon biscuits and her freshly churned peach ice cream.

There was something both quaint and deeply touching about these Sunday afternoon teas. We don't have silver teas anymore, but I keep gathering recipes as if the next one were just around the corner. A tart summer green-apple pie would be perfect, I find myself thinking. I know Aunt Vestula would approve.

THE RECIPES

Lemon Biscuits
Best Iced Tea Ever
Creamy Peach Ice Cream
Summer Green-Apple Pie

LEMON BISCUITS
Makes 12 to 15

These light, sconelike biscuits are delicious served with hot tea or ice cream.

2 cups all-purpose flour
4 tablespoons sugar
4 teaspoons baking powder
⅛ teaspoon salt
¼ cup chilled butter, cut into 8 pieces
2 tablespoons fresh lemon juice
6 tablespoons heavy cream
2 large eggs, lightly beaten
The grated rind of 1 lemon

1. Preheat oven to 400° F.

2. In a large bowl, sift together the flour, 2 tablespoons of the sugar, the baking powder, and the salt. Using a pastry blender, cut in the butter until the mixture resembles coarse cornmeal.

3. In a small bowl, combine the lemon juice, 4 tablespoons of the cream, the eggs, and the grated lemon rind and mix well.

4. Make a well in the center of the flour mixture, pour in the wet mixture, and stir with a few quick strokes, mixing just until the dry ingredients are moistened.

5. Turn the dough out onto a floured surface. Use your hands to pat the dough to a thickness of about ¾ inch, then use a rolling pin to roll

gently to about ⅜-inch thickness. Be careful to handle the dough as little as possible.

6. Cut the dough into biscuit rounds about 1 ¼ inches in diameter and place on an ungreased baking sheet. Brush with the 2 remaining tablespoons of cream and sprinkle with the 2 remaining tablespoons of sugar. Bake in the preheated oven for 12 to 15 minutes or until the biscuit tops are light gold. Serve warm.

BEST ICED TEA EVER
Makes 2 quarts

This recipe, given to me by my cousin Lottie, is the very best version of our Southern "sweet" iced tea that I've ever found. The lemons make it tart enough even for Northerners. Be sure to remove the rind from the lemon (a potato peeler makes it easy) before squeezing out the juice.

1 "running over" cup sugar
2 quarts cold water
The juice and rind (in strips) of 2 lemons
5 regular tea bags

1. Combine the sugar, water, and lemon juice in a large saucepan and bring to a boil over high heat, stirring frequently. Remove from heat.

2. Add the lemon rind and tea bags, cover the pan, and allow to steep for 20 minutes.

3. Strain the tea into a large pitcher, chill, and serve.

CREAMY PEACH ICE CREAM
Sorry, but it serves only 3

This is a summer favorite that we make from any—actually, all—of our farm's nine varieties of peaches. I think it's fine with any type of peach.

6 ripe fresh peaches, peeled, pitted, and quartered
1 tablespoon plus about ¾ cup sugar
2 teaspoons fresh lemon juice
2 cups milk
2 cups light cream
4 large egg yolks
2 tablespoons vanilla extract

1. In a food processor or blender, puree the peaches. Place the puree in a small bowl, add 1 tablespoon sugar and the lemon juice, and mix well. Set aside.

2. In a medium saucepan, combine the milk and light cream and cook over medium-low heat just until small bubbles appear at the edges. Remove from heat.

3. In a medium bowl, combine the egg yolks and remaining ¾ cup sugar. Return the milk mixture to a simmer, then add about 1 cup of it to the egg mixture, whisking constantly. Pour this mixture back into the saucepan with the rest of the milk mixture, return it to the stove, and cook over low heat, stirring constantly with a wooden spoon until the mixture is thick enough to coat the back of the spoon, about 5 minutes.

4. Remove mixture from heat, stir in vanilla extract, and freeze in an ice cream maker according to the manufacturer's instructions.

Wild Fruit

In the old days, everybody had a pear tree, or a peach tree, or an apple tree, or some kind of fruit tree in the backyard for food. We were always sticking something in the ground and hoping it would grow. I remember my mama planted plum trees in the flower bed right next to the front porch. When they matured, she could sit right there in her rocking chair and reach the ripe plums.

Of course, back then there were wild fruit trees, too. They had smaller fruit, but it was still sweet and delicious. Sometimes in the fall when my brothers Jack and Orestus were pruning peach trees, they would come across a wild seckel pear tree and they'd fill their pockets with those delicious little pears to eat during the day.

Today you can still find wild pears on our farm, right beside the road that leads down to the fishpond. I like to take visitors there so they can get an idea of why we are still so grateful for whatever the land gives us.

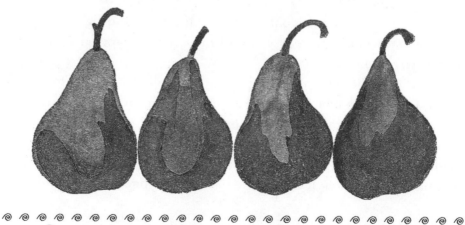

SUMMER GREEN-APPLE PIE

Makes one 9-inch pie

The apple trees that grow in people's backyards offer the best-tasting green apples for this pie. Usually these apples don't have any particular name but they do have the most wonderful flavor. If you have to buy your apples, Granny Smiths work best for this recipe.

¾ cup sugar

2 tablespoons all-purpose flour

½ teaspoon ground cinnamon

⅛ teaspoon freshly grated nutmeg

⅛ teaspoon salt

½ teaspoon grated orange peel

5 to 6 medium tart green apples, peeled,
cored, and cut into ¼-inch slices

¼ cup chilled unsalted butter, cut into small pieces

Pastry for a 2-crust 9-inch pie (page 81)

1. Preheat oven to 400° F.

2. In a large bowl, combine the sugar, flour, cinnamon, nutmeg, and salt and mix well. Add the orange peel and apples and mix lightly.

3. Heap the apple mixture into a pie plate lined with unbaked crust, dot the mixture with the butter pieces, and top with the second crust. Trim edges of the top and bottom crusts to ¾ inch, press the edges together lightly, fold under, and seal. Flute with fingers or crimp with a fork. With a paring knife, cut small slits near the center of the top crust for vents.

4. Bake on the center rack in the preheated oven for 20 minutes. Remove and cover edges of crust with foil. Return to oven and bake an additional 30 to 40 minutes or until well browned and bubbly. Cool on a wire rack and serve while still warm.

Miss Hattie's Hurricane Survival Fireplace Dinner

In September 1989, Hurricane Hugo cut an unexpected and devastating path through York County, South Carolina. Among other things, it knocked out electrical power all over the county.

After several days without electricity, real hunger for hot food started to settle in, along with the fear that I would lose the entire contents of my refrigerator and deep freezer.

Remembering that Miss Hattie, a longtime friend and neighbor, had a wood-burning cookstove, I gathered up some eggs, an unopened quart of buttermilk, and some still-frozen chicken drumsticks and headed for her house. It turned out I wasn't alone. Several other women had the same idea and we all gathered in Miss Hattie's living room. There was a crackling fire blazing in her fireplace, but the cookstove was cold: it no longer had a flue and could not be used.

But there was still that fire, and fortunately Miss Hattie had held on to every kettle and long-handled black cast-iron skillet her mama had ever owned. So we pooled our water—yes, water was scarce; we had our wells, but they didn't pump water without electricity—and everyone pitched in to help clean those ancient kettles and skillets.

The absence of a hook in her wide-open fireplace on which to hang a kettle didn't seem to bother Miss Hattie. She poked through her hurricane-swept yard and collected bricks and rocks on which to perch the skillets and kettles safely over the hot fireplace coals. Eager helpers kept the firewood in full supply.

Miss Hattie cooked the meal in stages, and so we found ourselves eating that way, too. First she lightly browned sage-seasoned chicken legs and onions in one of the large lidded skillets. When browned, she removed them and placed them in a smaller skillet and covered them to keep them warm. Using the large skillet again, Miss Hattie added oil and browned pork steaks seasoned with garlic and pepper. Once the steaks had been turned, she placed the chicken legs and onions on top of them, then covered the skillet to cook over slow coals in a corner of the fireplace.

Over hotter coals, Miss Hattie browned buttermilk dumplings for a skillet-fried blackberry and dumpling dessert. She put the finished dumplings in an empty turkey roasting pan set on the hearth and covered them, but they were so delicious that only a few from each batch ever made it to the roasting pan.

Using the one remaining empty kettle, Miss Hattie opened and cooked some of her home-canned vegetable soup. A quart of home-canned string beans was also opened and served, accompanied by home-made squash pickles and some okra pickles seasoned with garlic.

Outside the winds were still. The rain had finally stopped. It was still cold and wet but we were warm and so we lingered on. Miss Hattie buried sweet potatoes in the hot ashes to bake. Later we slit them open and ate them topped with cinnamon-honey butter and hot pepper jelly.

We talked about how the old people used to put crisply fried fatback meat, also called salt pork, on sweet potatoes and topped them with a sprinkling of pepper. Some people didn't use the meat, but rather its rendered fat to fry onions and peppers that they piled on top of the potatoes along with a big spoonful of clabbered cream.

At the corner of the fireplace hearth, one of Miss Hattie's handmade straw brooms, made from sedge that grows wild in the fields, stood wedged into a peck peach basket half filled with large, ripe wild muscadines gathered just before the hurricane. There Miss Hattie was, continuing life at the pace of times gone by. The house itself provided a sojourn into the past.

Miss Hattie talked about the "good old days," the quilting bees she used to enjoy so much, her long-held wish for a large wood-burning cookstove like the one her mother had. I listened, and in the cozy warmth of Miss Hattie's home, I shared her wish. I vowed I'd never again be totally dependent on electricity.

A few months later I made good on my vow: I had my bricked-up fireplace reopened so I could always cook and heat with wood if necessary. But guess what? After a couple winter seasons of cleaning out fireplace ashes, I had gas logs installed. But even my modern fireplace stirs memories of that hurricane dinner with Miss Hattie and the comfort we felt around her log-warmed hearth, and I'm reminded of the old-time ways.

THE RECIPES

Kettle-Braised Chicken and Pork
Baked Sweet Potatoes with Onions and Peppers
Squash Pickles
Garlic Okra Pickles
Skillet Blackberries and Dumplings

KETTLE-BRAISED CHICKEN AND PORK

Serves 4 to 6

If you add potatoes and carrots to this recipe, the dish becomes a hearty winter meal all by itself. I have modified the recipe a bit from the way my friend Miss Hattie prepared it, but it still makes a wonderful hearth supper when cooked in an open fireplace.

8 pieces of chicken (thighs, breasts, or legs)
1 ½ pounds boneless pork chops, cut into ½-inch strips
2 tablespoons minced fresh sage (1 tablespoon dried)
3 tablespoons vegetable oil
1 medium onion, chopped
3 cloves garlic, minced
1 teaspoon salt, or to taste
1 teaspoon freshly ground black pepper, or to taste
½ cup chicken stock (you can substitute water)

1. Wipe the chicken and pork with a clean, damp cloth and rub all over with the sage.

2. In a large, heavy cast-iron kettle, heat the oil over medium-high heat until hot but not smoking. Add the onion and cook, stirring occasionally, until just transparent, about 5 minutes. Add the garlic and cook, stirring frequently, another 2 minutes.

3. Add the chicken and pork and cook until lightly browned, about 10 minutes, turning to brown all sides.

4. Season to taste with salt and pepper and add the chicken stock. Gently move the chicken and pork to the sides of the kettle, scoop up the onions and garlic from the kettle bottom, and place on top of the pork and chicken. Cover, reduce heat to low, and cook for 45 to 50 minutes or until pork is tender and chicken shows no trace of pink near the bone. Serve at once.

BAKED SWEET POTATOES WITH ONIONS AND PEPPERS
Serves 2

This meatless treat is hearty enough for a main course. If you feel the need for meat, though, go ahead and crumble some crisp-fried bacon into the vegetable mixture. If you want to make it like the old-timers did, substitute rendered pork fat for the olive oil.

2 medium sweet potatoes
1 tablespoon olive oil
1 medium onion, thinly sliced
1 medium red, yellow, or green bell pepper, seeded and thinly sliced
⅛ teaspoon salt, or to taste
⅛ teaspoon freshly ground black pepper, or to taste
3 tablespoons clotted or sour cream
1 tablespoon chopped fresh chives or scallion tops

1. Preheat oven to 400° F.

2. Wash and dry the potatoes and pierce them several times with a fork. Place them in a small, shallow baking pan and bake for 40 to 45 minutes or until they are easily pierced with a fork but still offer some resistance.

3. Meanwhile, in a medium-size heavy skillet, heat the olive oil over medium heat until hot but not smoking. Add the onions and peppers and saute, stirring occasionally, until tender, about 8 to 10 minutes. Season with salt and pepper.

4. Remove the potatoes from the oven and cut in half. Transfer the potatoes to a serving plate, spoon the onions and peppers on top, and serve hot, accompanied by sour cream and chives.

SQUASH PICKLES
Makes about 9 pints

These pickles are very easy to make, a good way to use that superabundant garden supply of squash. I think yellow squash makes the prettiest pickles, but you can use other types of squash, too. Can them in decorative half-pint glass jars and you'll always have a little gift ready to take with you when you're invited to a friend's house for a meal.

4 quarts small, thinly sliced fresh yellow squash
(about 12 small squash)
2 quarts thinly sliced onions
(about 6 medium onions)
½ cup salt
2 quarts crushed ice
5 cups sugar
5 cups white distilled vinegar
1 ½ teaspoons turmeric
1 tablespoon mustard seed
1 tablespoon celery seed

1. In a stockpot, combine the squash, onion, salt, and ice, mix gently, and allow to stand for 3 hours. Drain, wash thoroughly in cold water, and drain again.

2. In a large saucepan, combine the sugar, vinegar, turmeric, mustard seed, and celery seed and cook over medium-high heat, stirring constantly, until the first bubbles of a simmer begin to appear. Remove from heat immediately.

3. Pack the squash-onion mixture into hot, sterilized Ball Mason jars and add hot syrup to cover, leaving a ¼-inch space at the top of each jar. Wipe the jar rims with a clean, damp cloth, fit them with hot lids, and tightly screw on the metal rings. Process in a bath of boiling water for 10 minutes (the water should cover the jars by about 1 inch), cool on a wire rack, and store in a cool, dark place.

GARLIC OKRA PICKLES
Makes 4 pints

These simple but tasty okra pickles can be served as a condiment at any meal. They are also nice in salads.

3 pounds uncut fresh okra
3 cups water
1 cup white distilled vinegar
¼ cup pickling (kosher) salt
3 cloves garlic, crushed

1. Wash okra, trim off stems, but do not cut into the pods themselves. Drain and pack into 4 hot, sterilized pint Ball Mason jars.

2. In a medium saucepan, combine the water, vinegar, salt, and garlic and bring to a boil over medium-high heat. Pour immediately into the jars, filling to within ½ inch of the top.

3. Wipe the jar rims with a clean, damp cloth, fit them with hot lids, and tightly screw on the metal rings. Process in a boiling-water bath for 5 minutes (the water should cover the jars by about 1 inch), counting from when the water returns to a boil after the jars are immersed. Cool on a wire rack and store in a cool, dark place.

SKILLET BLACKBERRIES AND DUMPLINGS

Serves 4 to 6

This delicious dessert can be made on top of a stove or in a heavy cast-iron skillet over hot coals. You won't find a better dessert for a cookout or camping trip.

1 cup all-purpose flour
1 ½ teaspoons baking powder
½ teaspoon baking soda
½ teaspoon salt
2 teaspoons plus 1 cup sugar
1 large egg, separated
⅔ cup buttermilk
3 tablespoons butter, melted
A pinch of ground nutmeg
1 quart fresh, canned, or frozen blackberries

1. In a small bowl, sift together the flour, baking powder, baking soda, salt, and 2 teaspoons of sugar.

2. In a large bowl, combine the egg yolk, buttermilk, 2 tablespoons of the butter, and the nutmeg and mix until well combined. Add these wet ingredients to the dry ingredients in 2 batches, mixing after each addition until just barely combined.

3. In a small bowl, beat the egg white until soft peaks form. Gently fold into the batter.

4. Use the remaining tablespoon of butter to grease a deep skillet at least 10 inches wide. Drop large spoonfuls of the dumpling batter into the skillet and cook, about 5 or 6 at a time, over medium-high heat, turning once, until both sides are browned, about 4 to 5 minutes per side. Remove from skillet and set aside. Continue this process until all the batter has been used up.

5. Pour the blackberries into the same skillet. Add the remaining cup of sugar (or less to taste if you are not a Southerner) and stir to combine. Bring to a simmer, reduce heat to low, place pan-fried dumplings on top, and cook, covered, for 10 minutes. Serve warm.

Early Recycling

In our family there was always a baby to be fed. Sometimes the baby was fed with a store-bought bottle, but more often we would take a clean soda pop bottle, wedge a nipple on top of it, and present that to the baby as its bottle.

Understand, though, that was the weekday bottle. It would be too embarrassing to take a bottle like that out on a Sunday, so we always had a store-bought bottle, too, which we held back for special occasions.

Because there was always a baby, there also were always empty formula cans around. If you cut them properly so they didn't have jagged edges—and believe me, my mama made sure they didn't—you could use them as cups. If we didn't have enough enameled tin cups for the workers, we would use these recycled cans when we brought them water during plowing, hoeing, and picking, or hot apple cider or sassafras tea at hog-killing time.

CHAPTER 14

Family Reunions

Summertime was special when I was a child. The peaches were ripe, the watermelons were ready, and kinfolk from all over were expected for the family reunion.

It was a busy time, getting the house ready for all the expected guests. Mama would select the best hens and fryers and pen them up so they wouldn't feed on wild garlic and onions. The cows, including my Starlight, were also specially tended—wild garlic and onion would ruin not only their milk but also the butter churned from it.

Daddy and my brothers would dig chalky clay from the creek beds to make whitewash. Everything from the fireplaces inside the house to the rocks around the flower beds outside received a fresh white coat in anticipation of the big event.

On the day before the reunion, long plank tables were built and placed out under the kudzu vine-covered trellis that my daddy had designed to run alongside our house. Then, with windows opened to let in the breeze, the cooking began.

A fire burned in the old wood stove all day and into the night. Cakes and pies emerged one after the other and were placed immediately in the "pie safe," a simple wooden cabinet that once stood in the corner of our dining room but was moved to the cooler back porch as soon as my daddy screened it in. True to its name, the cabinet kept pies—and cakes, too—safe not only from flies and other insects but from children as well. Its tin doors, perforated for ventilation, were always locked or securely fastened with a thin rope that defied our efforts to untie it—not that my cousins and I didn't try.

Family reunions lasted for days, and they were filled with feasting and the renewing of family ties. But as much fun as it was to have the reunions at our place, I looked forward even more to those reunions held at another relative's house. The cooking went on for days and nights before we were to leave. Then, in the early morning darkness, our large family piled into our old flatbed truck. Parents and grandparents squeezed into the cab of the truck, children and food were in the back on the open bed. The smell of warm food mingling with the cool, fresh predawn air set the stage for an exciting day.

Now years later, my sisters and I still work late into the night getting ready for family reunions. We try to figure out how some of the traditional, heavenly tasting foods were made. We always talk about Aunt Vestula's cooking and try out seasonings—a dash of this, a pinch of that, a smidgen of something else. We try to remember, but as the night turns into early morning, we begin to have trouble remembering even Aunt Vestula, much less her recipes.

Yes, family-reunion cooking can be intense. The competition is keen, the demand for originality high. We all want to outdo each other. In the end, though, it all comes together. Somebody always makes the traditional foods. I'll use an old family recipe for chicken and dumplings.

Another relative will bring deviled eggs with caper stuffing, another will arrive with a celery cake. These dishes remind the gathered relatives never to forget the past and always, always to expect some bitter with the sweet, a caution of long standing among African-Americans in the South.

At a recent reunion, one cousin followed a really old tradition. Wearing a long flowered dress and a flower-covered straw hat, she circulated among the relatives, handing out pretty handwritten recipes for all the foods she had brought and inviting everyone to dine at her table.

Other relatives also carry on family traditions. An aged cousin's son makes hoecakes just the way his father did each year at the reunion — with a loose cornmeal batter cooked on a hoe held above the hot coals of a dying fire. Relatives wait patiently for the hoecakes to brown, then line up for my brother Orestus's famous oxtail soup. I watch Uncle John Luke's great-grandson take a second helping of crisply fried cooter (that's what we call green turtle), but he doesn't know how to tell the story my uncle told every year: "The cooter has the taste of forty different kinds of meat . . ." (Each time Uncle John Luke told the story, the number of meats increased.) And the great-grandson can't offer my uncle's firsthand knowledge of making mead, nor can he play a song on a corncob flute or a homemade harmonica. I miss Uncle John Luke.

I settle down on a burlap-covered bale of freshly cut hay and watch the dancing. I'm tempted to join in but instead take a final offering of homemade lemon ice cream and a slice of warm apple bread pudding. Flashing lightning bugs provide country-style strobe lights for the dancers. I listen to more stories, more memories, and I, too, remember.

At day's end, as city relatives load up their expensive grills, they study my homemade model — an old oven rack mounted on rocks encircling a bed of lively coals. It may be unsophisticated, but, like many simple things, it does the job. In the country, that's all that really counts.

THE RECIPES

Caper-Stuffed Eggs
Peanut Soup
Orestus's Oxtail Soup
Southern-Style Chicken and Dumplings
Fried Okra and Potatoes
Celery Cake
"No Regrets" Apple Bread Pudding
Fresh Lemon Ice Cream

CAPER-STUFFED EGGS

Serves 6

Our family has used capers in its cooking for as long as I can remember. Family lore has it that Aunt Vestula brought the idea from South Carolina's Low Country on one of her visits. These caper-stuffed eggs are a favorite appetizer at family reunions.

6 hard-boiled eggs
1 tablespoon finely chopped fresh chives
1 tablespoon mayonnaise
1 teaspoon Dijon mustard
1 teaspoon garlic oil (page 170)
1 teaspoon red wine vinegar
2 teaspoons capers, chopped
Salt and freshly ground black pepper to taste

1. Peel the eggs and cut them in half crosswise. Remove yolks and place whites in a bowl filled with ice water to firm and brighten them.

2. In a small bowl, use a wooden spoon to mash the yolks. Add the chives, mayonnaise, mustard, garlic oil, and vinegar and mix well. Stir in the capers and season to taste with salt and pepper.

3. Drain the egg whites and pat dry with paper towels. Place the whites cut side up in a clean egg carton to hold them steady and fill the cavities with the egg yolk mixture. Cover the carton tightly with aluminum foil and refrigerate until ready to serve.

PEANUT SOUP

Serves 4

The nutty taste of peanuts, which we Southerners call groundnuts, combines with sweet potatoes to give this hearty soup a special flavor. Make sure that you chop the peanuts very finely so that they thicken the soup as well as add flavor.

2 tablespoons butter
1 large sweet potato, peeled and cubed
½ cup roughly chopped celery
½ cup roughly chopped onions
2 tablespoons minced fresh parsley
2 tablespoons all-purpose flour
One 20-ounce can stewed tomatoes, undrained
4 cups chicken stock
2 cups finely chopped peanuts
Salt and freshly ground black pepper to taste
Minced green onions and chopped peanuts for garnish (optional)

1. In a large, heavy saucepan, melt the butter over medium heat. Add the sweet potato, celery, onion, and parsley. Sprinkle the flour over the vegetables and stir in while cooking. Continue to cook, stirring occasionally, until the vegetables are tender, about 12 to 15 minutes.

2. Meanwhile, in a separate saucepan, combine the tomatoes and stock and bring to a simmer over medium-high heat. Stir in the vegetables and peanuts and season to taste with salt and pepper. Turn heat to low and simmer for about 20 minutes, stirring occasionally. Adjust seasoning and, if desired, sprinkle with green onions and additional chopped peanuts before serving.

Cooters

We didn't use to have fishponds on our farm like we do today. But, oh, we had fishing holes, creeks, and streams teeming with fresh fish, fat frogs, and, best of all, green turtles, which we call cooters. Cooters are good eating, and we still catch and cook them.

Cooking a cooter is some work. After you catch it, you put it in a small barrel of water taken from the pond or creek where you caught it. When you're ready to cook it, you poke a sturdy stick into the barrel. The cooter will snap onto it and then you can pull him from the barrel. No, he is not likely to let go. Next, remove the head with a sharp axe or hatchet. When the body is still, cut the flesh from the shell with a sharp knife. The claws and rubbery-textured skin then have to be removed from the flesh and discarded. At this point, you cut the cooter meat into pieces, wash it thoroughly in saltwater, rinse it, and then parboil it to tenderize it. After being parboiled, the cooter can be roasted, fried, or further boiled, depending on your recipe.

It has always been said that cooter meat has the combined taste of many different types of wild game, fish, and seafood. The number of combined tastes varies from Southern state to Southern state. In Filbert, South Carolina, the latest count by my brother Orestus puts the number of different tastes in cooter meat at forty. So I guess it is worth the effort of cooking it, after all.

Garlic Oil

In the old days, farm households stocked lots of garlic. There was wild garlic in the fields, and most farmers planted garlic in their vegetable gardens, too. Many farm children wore garlic necklaces—a few cloves of garlic threaded onto a heavy string—to ward off the common cold. We had lots of garlic in our home, but I'm grateful it was never used in that way. Our garlic was used strictly for cooking.

Today I often use garlic *oil* for cooking. It's so easy to make. You just peel and mash three cloves of garlic, put them in a sterilized pint jar, and fill up the jar with olive or vegetable oil. If you keep the jar tightly sealed in a cool, dark place, the oil will last for months. It's an easy country way to add garlic flavor in a second, especially to fried chicken and pork chops.

ORESTUS'S OXTAIL SOUP

6 to 8 hearty servings

The whole family reaps the rewards for its hard work on the farm when my brother Orestus uses our own fresh vegetables for his famous oxtail soup. It may seem a little tedious to brown each ingredient before it goes into the pot, but the flavor is well worth the effort.

4 tablespoons vegetable oil
2 to 3 pounds oxtails
2 tablespoons plus 1 teaspoon all-purpose flour
10 cups beef stock or water
4 cups chopped onions (3 to 4 large onions)
4 large cloves garlic, chopped
1 ½ cups white or sweet potatoes, peeled and chopped
into bite-size pieces
1 to 2 pounds beef short ribs
1 cup chopped fresh parsley
1 cup freshly shelled green field peas (black-eye,
purple hull, or colossus), rinsed and drained
1 cup freshly cut corn kernels (about 2 ears)
1 cup fresh okra, thinly sliced
1 tablespoon minced fresh basil
1 tablespoon minced fresh sage
½ teaspoon freshly ground black pepper, or to taste
½ teaspoon minced fresh chili pepper, or to taste
2 pounds ripe fresh tomatoes, chopped (3 to 4 large tomatoes)
1 ½ cups shredded cabbage
A dash of sugar
Salt to taste

1. In a 6-quart saucepan, heat 2 tablespoons of the oil over medium heat until it begins to dance a little. Add the oxtails a few at a time in a single layer. After putting the oxtails in the pan, sprinkle them very lightly with flour (using a total of 2 tablespoons for *all* the meat) and brown lightly on both sides, about 3 minutes per side. Remove from pan and place on paper towels to drain. Repeat process until all oxtails are browned (you shouldn't have to add more oil between batches).

2. Drain the oil from the saucepan and put all the oxtails back in it. Add the beef stock or water, making sure that the oxtails are submerged, and bring to a boil over high heat. Reduce heat to low and simmer for 2 ½ hours or until the oxtails are tender, adding more stock or water as needed.

3. After the oxtails have been simmering for 2 hours, begin preparing the vegetables and short ribs. In a medium skillet, heat 2 teaspoons of oil over medium heat until it just starts to dance. Add the onions and garlic and saute, stirring occasionally, until the onions are limp, about 7 minutes. Add the onions and garlic to the simmering oxtails. Add another 2 teaspoons of oil to the skillet and again heat until it begins to dance. Add the potatoes, sprinkle with 1 teaspoon flour, and cook, turning as needed, until lightly browned on all sides, about 6 minutes. When browned, add to the oxtails. Add the final 2 teaspoons of oil to the skillet and again heat until it begins to dance. Add the short ribs in a single layer (in batches if necessary) and brown lightly, about 2 minutes per side. Add to the oxtails.

4. Now add to the oxtail mixture the parsley, peas, corn, okra, basil, sage, black pepper, and chili pepper. Stir to mix and continue to simmer over low heat, covered, for 25 to 30 minutes.

5. Skim the fat from the surface of the broth, then add the tomatoes and their juice, the cabbage, the sugar, and salt to taste. Continue to simmer, covered, for about 30 minutes, stirring occasionally, until the meat is very tender and the vegetables are cooked through. Serve hot.

SOUTHERN-STYLE CHICKEN AND DUMPLINGS
Serves 6 to 8

This old family recipe was a favorite Sunday meal that provided a homey flavor on many a cold winter day.

1 whole 4-pound chicken, cleaned and lightly rubbed with salt
2 onions, roughly chopped
2 stalks celery, roughly chopped
1 small peeled sweet potato (you can substitute a carrot)
1 clove garlic, peeled
⅛ teaspoon salt
2 teaspoons ground white pepper
1 bay leaf

For the dumplings:

2 cups all-purpose flour
1 teaspoon salt
3 teaspoons baking powder
⅔ cup milk

1. In a large saucepan or stockpot, combine the whole chicken, 3 quarts water, and the onions, celery, sweet potato, garlic, salt, pepper, and bay leaf. Cover and bring to a boil over medium-high heat. Reduce heat to low and simmer for about 2 hours or until chicken is very tender. Remove chicken and drain well, setting the stock aside.

2. When chicken is cool enough to handle, remove the skin and discard. Remove the meat from the bones, discard the bones, and set the meat aside.

3. Strain the stock and add water if necessary to make 3 quarts.

4. For the dumplings, sift together in a large bowl the flour, salt, and baking powder. Stir in the milk until just blended. Turn the dough out onto a floured surface and knead until firm. Cover and allow to stand at room temperature for 30 minutes.

5. Roll the dough out to a thickness of about ⅛ inch and cut into 1" x 3" strips. Allow to sit, uncovered, for about 45 minutes so that when cooked they do not puff but stay flat like noodles.

6. Bring the strained stock to a boil over high heat. Add the dumplings a few at a time, bringing the stock back to a boil after each addition. Reduce heat to low, cover the pot, and simmer for 15 minutes. Stir in the chicken meat and serve.

FRIED OKRA AND POTATOES

Serves 4

Finely chopped onion makes an excellent addition to this simple but tasty vegetable dish. Just add it to the pan with the okra and potatoes after the oil is properly heated.

¼ cup all-purpose flour
1 tablespoon white or yellow cornmeal
Salt and freshly ground black pepper to taste
1 pound fresh okra, washed, stemmed, and cut crosswise
into ½-inch slices
½ cup diced potatoes (about 1 medium potato)
Vegetable oil for frying

1. In a shallow dish, combine the flour, cornmeal, salt, and pepper. Dredge the okra and potatoes in this mixture.

2. In a large, heavy skillet, heat about ½ inch of oil over medium-high heat until hot but not smoking. Place the vegetables in the skillet, reduce heat to medium, and cook, covered, until the vegetables are tender, about 10 minutes, turning frequently.

3. Remove cover and cook an additional 2 minutes to brown more. Serve at once.

CELERY CAKE
Serves 8 to 10

For many years there was no written recipe for this cake. Our cousin who always brought the cake to family reunions refused to tell what was in her "vegetable cake." Finally, through numerous trial and error attempts, we came up with this recipe, which I think duplicates her moist and delicious cake almost exactly.

3 cups all-purpose flour
2 teaspoons baking powder
½ teaspoon salt
2 teaspoons ground cinnamon
2 large eggs, lightly beaten
1 ½ cups sugar
1 teaspoon vanilla extract
1 cup mayonnaise
½ cup milk
2 ½ cups peeled, diced apples
1 cup coarsely chopped walnuts
½ cup finely diced celery

1. Preheat oven to 350° F.

2. In a medium bowl, sift together the flour, baking powder, salt, and cinnamon. Set aside.

3. In a large bowl, cream the eggs, sugar, and vanilla, beating until the mixture is light and fluffy (at least 2 minutes with an electric beater, much longer by hand). Beat in the mayonnaise.

4. Add a third of the flour mixture to the egg-sugar mixture followed by half the milk. Mix to combine after each addition. Repeat this process, ending with the final third of the flour mixture.

5. Using a large wooden spoon or rubber spatula, mix in the apples, walnuts, and celery until evenly distributed.

6. Turn the batter into a greased and floured 12-cup fluted tube pan (about 9 inches in diameter). Bake in the preheated oven for about 1 hour to 1 hour and 10 minutes or until a knife inserted into the cake comes out clean. Cool cake in the pan on a wire rack for 10 minutes, then loosen edges and turn out on a rack to cool completely.

Canning Time

In late summer, my mama would begin canning in earnest. Sometimes her sisters would come from the city to help, and they would bring their children along. These visits were the only vacations my city cousins ever had.

What fun-filled days they were. My cousins and I would hang around doing small chores, hunting for small flat stones that wouldn't roll when we tossed them for hopscotch, and waiting for a taste of someone's prized wild blackberry or plum jelly before it reached the jars. Freshly made jelly, barely cooled, spooned onto hot buttered biscuits—nothing could be better. The fresh berry and plum juices stained not only our lips but our dresses as well. I will never forget the day my mama didn't notice I had on my Sunday dress. Oh, was she mad.

What happy days. Canning time wasn't just work for my mama and aunts; it was also a social event, almost like a quilting bee. For us children it was even better than the county fair.

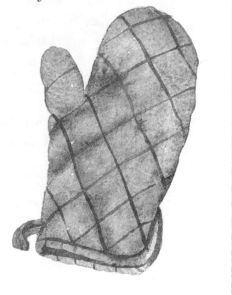

"NO REGRETS" APPLE BREAD PUDDING

Serves 6 to 8

This recipe got its name because you will have no regrets for either the calories or the labor involved in making it.

5 ½ tablespoons unsalted butter, softened
2 Granny Smith or other tart cooking apples
The juice of ½ lemon
¼ teaspoon ground nutmeg
¼ teaspoon ground cinnamon
1 tablespoon plus 1 cup sugar
5 slices of good-quality white bread, each slice about ⅓ inch thick
2 tablespoons dark raisins, soaked in boiling water
for 10 minutes, then drained
¼ cup roughly chopped walnuts or pecans
2 whole eggs plus 2 egg yolks
2 cups light cream
A pinch of salt
1 teaspoon lemon extract
½ teaspoon vanilla extract

1. Smear ½ tablespoon of softened butter on the inside of a 10" x 7" x 2" baking dish. Set aside.

2. Preheat oven to 350° F.

3. Peel and core the apples, cut into very thin slices, and toss in the lemon juice. In a heavy skillet, melt 2 tablespoons of butter over moderate heat, add the apples, and saute until just tender, about 10 to 12 minutes, stirring occasionally. Remove skillet from heat, stir in the nutmeg, cinnamon, and 1 tablespoon of sugar, and set aside.

4. Remove the crusts from the bread. Spread the remaining 3 tablespoons of softened butter evenly over the bread. Arrange bread in a single layer on the bottom of the buttered baking dish, overlapping the edges of the bread slightly. Over the bread scatter the raisins, nuts, and sauteed apples with all the pan juices.

5. In a small bowl, beat together the whole eggs and the yolks. Beat the remaining 1 cup sugar into the eggs.

6. In a heavy saucepan, combine the cream and salt and scald over moderate heat. When tiny bubbles form around the edges of the cream, remove from heat and strain by small amounts into the egg mixture, stirring to combine after each addition. Stir in the lemon and vanilla extracts. Strain this mixture over the bread and apples, pushing down the edges of the bread to cover completely with the egg-cream mixture.

7. Place the baking dish in a large roasting pan and fill the roasting pan with enough hot water to come a third of the way up the baking dish. Bake in the preheated oven for 40 to 45 minutes or until a knife inserted in the center of the pudding comes out clean. Place on a wire rack to cool and serve warm or cold.

FRESH LEMON ICE CREAM
Serves 2

This ice cream will keep its flavor for a while if you pack it firmly in a small metal bowl, cover it tightly first with plastic wrap and then with foil, and put it in the freezer. It's so delicious, though, I doubt you'll have any left over.

1 tablespoon lemon zest
¼ cup fresh lemon juice
1 cup sugar
2 cups light cream (or 1 cup heavy cream plus 1 cup milk)
⅛ teaspoon salt
A few drops of yellow food coloring (optional)

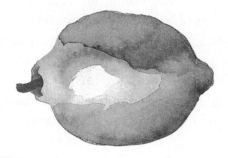

1. In a large bowl, combine the lemon zest, lemon juice, and sugar and stir to combine well.

2. Gradually add the cream, salt, and, if desired, the food coloring, stirring constantly. Continue to stir until sugar is dissolved.

3. Pour the mixture into ice cube trays with the dividers removed or into an 8" x 8" metal baking pan. Cover tightly with foil and freeze until the mixture is solid around the edges and mushy in the middle. Stir well with a wooden spoon, cover with foil, and continue to freeze until completely firm.

Cooking for Northerners

N ews that relatives were coming down from Up North was always cause for immediate action in our family. My mama would hurriedly select the best chickens for special feeding; a big ham saved expressly for company would be brought in from the smokehouse; and the supply of pickles, preserves, and jams would be checked to be sure we had enough of each variety.

On the day the company from Up North arrived, the weekday flowered or checkered oil tablecloth was replaced by Sunday's pale blue damask tablecloth with matching napkins. We would open the windows to let in the breeze and set the table against a backdrop of summer sounds—the purr of a combine in the distant fields, the roar of a tractor bringing in a load of watermelons—Southern country summer sounds, sounds almost as delicious as our family's cooking.

Today I have countless relatives and friends who have moved Up North (some even have certified accents) and they visit me frequently. Judging from the foods they ask me to cook, I'm fully convinced that beneath their newly acquired taste for radicchio, what their taste buds really want is some down-home country cooking: field cress and pokeweed salad greens, buttermilk fried chicken, heavenly angel biscuits, hand-cranked peach ice cream. Or the fall foods — herbed pork roasts, wild persimmon pudding, vinegar pies, homemade butter stickies. No problem at all. I'm happy to oblige.

It was my writing activities, though, that introduced me to "true Northerners." These are folks who have never tasted the wonderful foods of the South, so when they visit me I want them to enjoy true Southern country cooking. But the words *gourmet* and *haute cuisine* always pop into my thoughts. I know that *gourmet* means a connoisseur of the delicacies of the table, and *haute cuisine* means fine cooking, food preparation as an art. I also know that both words can apply to Southern country cooking.

So how do I cook for Northerners? I'll let you in on a little secret: I cook the same foods I've cooked for years, only I may change the presentation, or the name, or the herbs. For example, when I make a vinegar pie with fresh fruit sauce, an old family favorite, I might strain the sauce through a sieve and call it a "coulis." When I fry up some okra, I'll use olive oil instead of vegetable oil and call it a "sauté." When I cook collard greens, I call them "winter greens." And if pressed for an exact name, I *never* say "karl-ards." Instead, I say "cawl-erds," all fancy like. Sometimes I sprinkle my "winter greens" with boiled fresh green peanuts, which have a flavor like pine nuts, or maybe with freshly grated Parmesan cheese. Can you believe that I've even started adding Parmesan to my black pepper cornbread, and sometimes to biscuits? I also cut down, way down, on the sugar for my Northern friends. Fresh minted sugarless iced tea always goes over big.

I must confess that during the course of experimenting with foods cooked "Northern-style," I have discovered a wider variety of fresh herbs. Now when I steam or stir fry mounds of fresh vegetables, I sprinkle them generously with fresh cilantro leaves, and I make a pork roast using fresh herbs instead of the dried herbs I used a few years ago.

So, when my Northern friends come to visit, I bake a batch of biscuits and borrow precious time to make a wild persimmon roll with cream cheese filling. I make sure my bottles of homemade herb vinegars and jars of pickles, jams, and relishes are proudly displayed on enamel and graniteware plates. For my table centerpieces, I simply roam the countryside, then place the flowers just as I picked them in pretty pitchers or rim-chipped, mismatched glasses and goblets that I'm still unable to throw out. Then I put on an apron—ironed but unstarched—and serve up, with a few new names and fancy extras, the simple, basic, healthy farm foods of the past. And you know what? When my guests are back Up North and they write me, the thing they always seem to remember best is the food.

THE RECIPES

Herbed Pork Roast
Yankee Okra
Fried Grits
Puffed Biscuits
Watermelon-Rind Pickles
Spiced Tomato Jam
Wild Persimmon Roll
Vinegar Pie with Strawberry Sauce

HERBED PORK ROAST

Serves 12

Fresh herbs give pork the taste of summer. You can serve this roast without the sauce if you want, but it's such an easy, quick, and delicious sauce, I figure you might as well make it.

One 7- to 8-pound pork roast, loin or fresh ham cut
2 tablespoons olive oil
2 tablespoons fresh lemon juice
1 tablespoon chopped fresh oregano
1 tablespoon chopped fresh thyme
1 tablespoon chopped fresh rosemary
1 tablespoon minced garlic
1 teaspoon salt, or to taste
1 teaspoon freshly ground black pepper, or to taste

For the sauce:

2 cups dry white wine
2 cups chicken or turkey stock
2 tablespoons minced onion or shallot

1. In a small bowl, mix together the olive oil, lemon juice, fresh herbs, garlic, salt, and pepper. Set the marinade aside.

2. Score the meaty side of the roast diagonally every 2 inches, about ½ inch deep. Rub the marinade over the meat, wrap tightly in plastic wrap or tin foil, and refrigerate overnight.

3. The next day, preheat oven to 350° F.

4. Unwrap the roast and place it on a rack in a medium-size roasting pan. Roast in the preheated oven for about 2 hours or until a thermometer inserted in the thickest part of the meat registers 155° F. Transfer the roast to a platter and cover loosely with foil. Leave the juices in the pan if you are going to make the sauce.

5. To make the sauce, remove the rack from the roasting pan and place the pan on a burner over medium-high heat. Add the wine, stock, and onion or shallot and bring to a boil, scraping up the brown bits from the bottom of the pan. Boil until reduced to about 2 cups. Strain, skim off fat, and serve sauce in a bowl or gravy boat along with the roast.

YANKEE OKRA
Serves 4 to 6 Northerners
or 2 Southerners

Prepared this way, okra is very healthful and doesn't have the slimy texture that Northerners hate so much. Try to get the small okra pods—they work best in this recipe.

1 pound okra pods, each less than 3 inches long
1 tablespoon olive oil
3 cloves garlic, minced
½ teaspoon red pepper flakes
1 teaspoon minced fresh thyme
1 teaspoon minced fresh basil
Salt and freshly ground black pepper to taste

1. Wash the okra, trim the stems, but leave on the caps.

2. In a large skillet, heat the olive oil over medium heat until hot but not smoking. Add the okra and saute, stirring occasionally, for 3 minutes.

3. Add the garlic, red pepper flakes, thyme, basil, and salt and pepper to taste. Cook for 1 minute more, stirring constantly. Remove from heat and serve immediately.

Okra

Okra is the best cash crop there is, because Southerners love it and they buy it no matter what. If you plant it by hand on the first warm day of late spring and are careful not to plant it deep in the soil like the tractor planter does, then you can be the first to harvest and sell it. At the beginning of the season, people are always willing to pay a higher price for it.

We wear gloves when harvesting okra pods, because the fibers on their outside are very much like fiberglass—you can't see the fibers, but by the time you've finished picking the okra, your hands will be full of them. We have more than three acres of okra, so we pick it by the bushelful.

These days, many of our customers are newly arrived Northerners who are vegetarians. I've introduced many a new customer to crowder peas, which are wonderful with a little fresh cilantro or some other fresh herb. Many of them are unfamiliar with okra as well. I give them recipes that involve breading and sauteing the okra, which keeps the vegetable from becoming "slimy." Of course, being a Southerner, I love the okra slime. I could sit there and eat it all day.

FRIED GRITS
Serves 6

One day at the farm stand, I overheard a Northerner—newly relocated to the South—say, "Down here it's not who you are that matters, it's knowing how to cook grits!" To me, learning how to cook grits means learning to care for others; loving grits means you have arrived. If you want to use instant grits for this recipe, skip the first step and make the grits according to the directions on the package, but remember to add the tablespoon of cornmeal when cooking the grits, as well as the sugar and nutmeg.

4 cups water
1 teaspoon salt, or to taste
1 cup uncooked grits (about 5 cups cooked)
1 tablespoon white cornmeal
⅛ teaspoon sugar
⅛ teaspoon nutmeg
1 tablespoon butter

1. In a medium saucepan, bring the water and salt to a boil. Stir in the grits and cornmeal, lower the heat, and cook slowly, stirring frequently, for about 40 minutes or until the mixture is thick like porridge. Stir in the sugar and nutmeg.

2. Pour cooked grits into a well-greased 8" x 4" loaf pan, cool to room temperature, then cover and refrigerate overnight.

3. Unmold the grits and cut into slices about ½ inch thick. In a heavy skillet, melt the butter over medium heat and fry the grits until golden on both sides, about 3 to 4 minutes per side. Serve piping hot with fresh homemade molasses or real maple syrup if you can get it.

PUFFED BISCUITS
Makes about 2 ½ dozen

Sometimes I make these biscuits kind of like a Middle Eastern griddle bread. After the first rise, I pinch off balls of the dough about two inches in diameter, roll them into round pancakes about six inches across, place them directly on the rack of a 450° F oven, and bake them for eight to ten minutes, turning them once with tongs. But no matter what the shape of these biscuits, I recommend you serve them warm with butter and fresh peach or cantaloupe slices. They will be a hit with Northerners and Southerners alike.

2 tablespoons active dry yeast
5 ½ cups sifted all-purpose flour
2 cups milk
3 tablespoons sugar
3 tablespoons shortening
2 teaspoons salt

1. Preheat oven to 350° F.
2. In a large bowl, combine the yeast and 2 cups of the flour.
3. In a medium saucepan, combine the milk, sugar, shortening, and salt and cook over medium heat, stirring constantly, just until the butter has melted.

4. Pour the milk mixture into the bowl with the flour mixture and beat to mix well. Continue to beat vigorously for about 3 minutes, scraping the sides and bottom of the bowl often. Stir in enough of the remaining 3 ½ cups of flour to make a moderately stiff dough.

5. Turn the dough out onto a floured surface and knead until smooth and elastic. Place in a greased bowl, turning once. Cover and let rise in a warm, draft-free place until double in size, about 45 minutes. Punch down, cover, and let rest 10 minutes.

6. Form the dough into balls about 1 ½ inches in diameter, roll each into a pancake about 3 inches in diameter, and place on an ungreased baking sheet. Bake in the preheated oven for 7 to 9 minutes or until puffed and lightly browned. Cool on a cloth-covered surface just until warm enough to handle, then serve at once.

WATERMELON-RIND PICKLES
Makes about 4 pints

When our sweet, thick-rind Congo watermelons are ripe, we try to savor every bit of the melon, including the rind—"waste not, want not."

4 quarts watermelon rind (the rind of 1 large watermelon)
2 tablespoons salt
1 quart white distilled vinegar
8 cups sugar
¼ cup crumbled cinnamon sticks
1 tablespoon whole cloves

1. Peel the green skin off the melon rind and trim off any remaining pink flesh. Cut into 1-inch squares and place in a large stockpot. Add the salt and enough boiling water to cover. Simmer over low heat until the rind is tender, about 15 to 20 minutes.

2. Drain the rind and chill in very cold water for at least 1 hour or overnight. When the rind has chilled, combine the vinegar and sugar in a stockpot and bring to a boil over high heat, stirring to be sure that the sugar dissolves completely. Reduce heat to low. Tie the cinnamon and cloves in a cheesecloth bag and add to the syrup.

3. Drain the rind, place in the syrup, and simmer over low heat until the rind becomes slightly transparent, about 30 minutes.

4. Remove the spice bag and pack the rind into hot, sterilized Ball Mason jars, leaving a ¼-inch space at the top of each jar. Wipe the jar rims with a clean, damp cloth, fit them with hot lids, and tightly screw on the metal rings. Process in a bath of boiling water for 10 minutes (the water should cover the jars by about 1 inch), cool on a wire rack, and store in a cool, dark place.

SPICED TOMATO JAM

Makes about 6 cups

This is a delicious condiment to make when the garden is overrun with ripe tomatoes. Both sweet and tart, it is wonderful served with meat or on top of baked sweet potatoes cut open and spread with a little butter.

5 ½ pounds ripe fresh tomatoes, peeled, seeded,
and cut into large chunks
2 lemons, very thinly sliced and seeds removed
3 cups sugar
½ cup honey
½ cup apple cider vinegar
½ cup water
1 teaspoon pickling (kosher) salt
½ teaspoon each: allspice, ground cloves,
ground ginger, and ground cinnamon
3 sticks cinnamon, each about 3 inches long

1. In an 8-quart stainless-steel pot, combine the tomatoes, lemon slices, sugar, honey, vinegar, water, and salt. Let stand for 1 hour at room temperature, stirring occasionally.

2. Stir in the allspice, cloves, ginger, and ground cinnamon. Let stand for 15 minutes at room temperature.

3. Set the pot over medium-high heat and bring to a boil, stirring occasionally. When the mixture begins to boil, tie the cinnamon sticks into a cheesecloth bag and add to the mixture. Continue to boil steadily, stirring frequently, until mixture has thickened, about 40 to 50 minutes. Stir the mixture constantly during the last 10 to 15 minutes to avoid scorching.

4. Discard the cinnamon sticks and immediately ladle the jam into hot, sterilized half-pint Ball Mason jars, filling to within ¼ inch of the top. Wipe the jar rims with a clean, damp cloth, fit them with hot lids, and tightly screw on the metal rings. Process in a bath of boiling water for 10 minutes (the water should cover the jars by about 1 inch), cool on a wire rack, and store in a cool, dark place.

Guests in the Kitchen

It doesn't seem to matter if the house is large or small, guests who stay longer than an hour or two tend to end up in the kitchen. I do not believe that "too many cooks spoil the broth." I believe they improve it.

My guests can leave their little black dresses and their suits and ties at home. The country life is far removed from formal city living, and in my scarce spare time I get ready for helping hands in the kitchen. I hand-sew patch-quilt aprons from leftover pieces of cloth or from old kitchen curtains and torn white sheets. Some aprons are hemmed, others aren't, depending on how much free time I have. I stack the aprons on a kitchen stool so guests can pick their favorite and then pitch in and help prepare the meal.

Everyone who cooks with me knows that when Dori cooks, perfection is pushed aside to concentrate on taste. So, if guests help cook and everything isn't perfect, we all share the blame. Most times, though, it seems that everyone shares congratulations on how good the food tastes.

WILD PERSIMMON ROLL

Serves 8 to 10

When the frost is on the wild persimmons, they are so sweet and flavorful that it's well worth the effort to gather them for puddings, pies, cakes, and ice cream. Wild persimmons are very small—it takes about two dozen of them to make one cup—and they are best gathered after a heavy frost. To prepare them, clean them well, remove the caps, and cut them in half. Then you can remove the seeds, scoop out the pulp, and mash it. Another way to prepare these little fruits is to remove the caps, soak the persimmons in sweet milk in the refrigerator for two hours, and then force them through a sieve. The pulp will come through the sieve and the seeds and skin will be left behind.

⅔ cup mashed wild persimmon pulp (about 16 persimmons)
¾ cup all-purpose flour
1 teaspoon baking powder
2 teaspoons ground cinnamon
1 teaspoon allspice
½ teaspoon ground nutmeg
½ teaspoon salt, or to taste
3 large eggs, lightly beaten
1 cup sugar
1 cup chopped pecans or walnuts
2 tablespoons confectioners' sugar
8 ounces cream cheese, softened
6 tablespoons unsalted butter, softened
1 teaspoon lemon extract

1. Preheat oven to 375° F. Grease a 15" x 10" x 1" jelly roll pan, line the pan with waxed paper, then grease the paper and dust with flour.

2. In a small, heavy saucepan, cook the persimmon pulp over medium heat, stirring constantly, until the pulp begins to bubble around the edges. Be careful not to boil. Set aside.

3. In a medium bowl, sift together the flour, baking powder, cinnamon, allspice, nutmeg, and salt. Set aside.

4. In a large bowl, beat the eggs and sugar together with an electric mixer until the mixture is light and custardlike and forms ribbons when the beaters are lifted, about 3 to 5 minutes. Beat in the cooked persimmon, then add the flour mixture and combine thoroughly.

5. Pour the batter into the jelly roll pan, smooth the surface with a rubber spatula, and, grasping the pan firmly with both hands, hold it 5 to 6 inches above the table and then smack it down onto the table to release any trapped air bubbles. Sprinkle the nuts evenly on top and bake in the preheated oven for 15 minutes or until the cake springs back when lightly touched in the center.

6. Remove the cake from the oven, handling it gently. Carefully loosen the edges with a knife. Sprinkle a clean, damp white tea towel with the confectioners' sugar, then turn the cake out on top of it, being very careful not to break the cake. Peel off the waxed paper and trim about ¼ inch from all sides of the cake to even it up. Fold one of the narrow ends of the towel up over the edge of the cake and roll up the towel and cake together. Place the cake seam down on a wire rack and allow it to cool completely.

7. In a medium bowl, beat together the cream cheese, butter, and lemon extract until smooth.

8. When the cake is cool, unroll it and spread the top with the cream cheese filling. Again starting from one of the narrow ends, roll the cake back up (this time without the towel) and refrigerate, seam side down, until ready to use. To serve, cut into rounds.

VINEGAR PIE WITH STRAWBERRY SAUCE
Makes one 9-inch pie

This recipe became a tradition in our family when a relative at one of the family reunions sought a new way to combine "the bitter with the sweet." The pie, which resembles a tart, needs to cook at low heat or the eggs will curdle. If you don't have any strawberries on hand, you can use peaches, raspberries, or blueberries for the sauce.

2 cups sugar
½ cup unsalted butter, softened
3 large eggs
2 tablespoons milk
2 tablespoons fresh lemon juice
2 tablespoons white distilled vinegar
2 tablespoons cornmeal
A pinch of all-purpose flour
2 scant teaspoons vanilla extract
1 unbaked 9-inch pie shell (page 81)

For the sauce:

1 cup fresh strawberries, washed, hulled, and halved
¼ cup cassis, triple sec, or other fruit liqueur

1. Preheat oven to 325° F.

2. In a medium bowl, cream the sugar and butter until light and fluffy. Add the eggs one at a time, mixing after each addition until well combined. Add the milk, lemon juice, vinegar, cornmeal, flour, and vanilla extract and mix well.

3. Pour the mixture into the unbaked pie shell and cook in the preheated oven for about 1 hour or until the custard is set and the top lightly browned. Cool on a wire rack.

4. In a small bowl, combine the strawberries and the liqueur and stir gently to mix.

5. Slice the pie and serve each slice topped with a couple tablespoons of the strawberry sauce.

CHAPTER 16

Unexpected Company

T rue Southern farmers had better stick to farming. They could never prosper from owning and operating bed-and-breakfast inns instead, because good old Southern hospitality means you cannot ask someone to pay for food eaten in your house.

Old-fashioned hospitality also dictates that if friends or neighbors are in your home around mealtime, you invite them to stay for a bite to eat. And, more often than not, the invitation is accepted. If you are in someone's home, you just kind of expect to eat with them if it's mealtime.

When I was a child, my favorite times were when kinfolk from the North visited. Expected or unexpected, my mama always managed to spread a feast.

It still happens to this day. Just this past year, on a blistering hot summer day around eleven in the morning, my brother Orestus and I were pleasantly surprised when kinfolk from Up North stopped by the farm stand. They were on their way to a funeral and were staying overnight at a nearby motel.

Now, if you live in Filbert, South Carolina, and have kin passing through, you've got to feed them a little something. So, during the slow noon hour at the farm stand, I slipped away to our family's fishpond, where I knew a neighbor was fishing. Even though the fish he had caught were technically ours, I bought the catfish from his bountiful morning catch, cleaned them, filleted them, and put them on ice.

That afternoon at the farm stand I stole away between customers to pick vegetables for supper, to prepare Silver Queen corn for roasting in the husk on the grill—and to threaten a work strike unless one of my brothers agreed to fire up our old grill and help me out. I left the farm stand a little early that day to visit my sister and beg her to help me get supper ready.

When our kin arrived at the house, my brother Orestus was wrapping fresh green cornhusks around the catfish, which I had already partially pan-cooked. He secured the cornhusks with strips of husk and put the wrapped fish on the hot grill to cook. He bragged that using cornhusks this way was an ancient cooking method that very, very few people knew about and even fewer could do well. Naturally, he didn't bother to tell them that, less than a mile away, the migrant Mexican peach pickers who had showed him how to do it in the first place were doubtless also roasting fish (along with mild chili peppers) in cornhusks.

While Orestus was tending the fish, my brother Jack showed up with his homemade beer bread. I made room on the grill for the corn to be roasted in its husks, then began the last-minute stir-fry of vegetables straight from the fields. It was all delicious, probably couldn't have been better if we had been planning it for a week.

Even after a hard day's work, we are usually not too tired to make homemade ice cream, but that day we were. For dessert, I cleared the table, spread it with sheets of colorful comic strips saved from the Sunday newspapers, and served chilled, crimson, sweet wedges of freshly pulled watermelon from our patch.

As fireflies lit up the early evening sky, there was happy talk and hearty laughter. Our guests departed early and we did not discourage them. The next day they had to travel and we had to work.

We didn't second-guess what our city kin said about the food after they left. My brother Jack poured water on the dying fire, Orestus started singing "The Peach-Picking Blues," and Virginia and I started to clean up. Another farming day was only hours away.

THE RECIPES

Cornhusk-Grilled Catfish
Grill-Roasted Corn on the Cob
"Pick of the Day" Stir-Fry Vegetables
Jack's Easy Beer Bread
Neighbor Cake

CORNHUSK-GRILLED CATFISH

Serves 8

For this recipe, the migrant Mexican peach pickers taught my brother Orestus that you need *fresh* cornhusks. You get them this way: peel the husks down to the stem of each ear of corn, being careful not to tear the husks. Then cut out the ear of corn with a knife, leaving the husks attached to each other at the base. Remove any remaining silk from inside the husks, cut a quarter-inch-wide strip from each husk to use as a tie, and immerse the husks in cold water for a half hour. I know it sounds like a lot of work, but it really isn't, and the flavor is worth it.

½ cup buttermilk
2 eggs
⅓ cup all-purpose flour
⅓ cup yellow cornmeal
1 teaspoon salt
1 teaspoon cayenne pepper
Eight 8-ounce catfish fillets
2 tablespoons vegetable oil
Freshly pulled cornhusks from 8 ears of corn,
soaking in cold water

1. In a shallow glass dish, beat together the buttermilk and eggs with a fork. In another shallow dish, combine the flour, cornmeal, salt, and cayenne pepper and mix well. Dip each fillet first in the milk mixture and then in the flour-cornmeal mixture, shaking off any excess coating.

2. In a large skillet, heat the oil over medium heat until hot but not smoking. Add the fillets and cook, turning only once, about 1 minute per side. Transfer fillets to a platter lined with paper towels and allow to drain.

3. Remove the cornhusks from the water and dry them with a towel. Place one partially cooked fillet in each cornhusk. Carefully fold the husks around the fillets, making sure the fillets remain flat, and tie the husks closed at the top with the reserved cornhusk strips.

4. Grill the husk-wrapped fish over a hot fire for 8 to 10 minutes or until the fillets are white all the way through. Serve at once.

GRILL-ROASTED CORN ON THE COB
Makes 1 dozen ears

The smoky, robust flavor of corn on the cob when cooked this way is far superior to the flavor of boiled corn. If you are concerned about fat, just discard the bacon before eating the corn.

1 dozen ears fresh corn, unshucked
24 strips hickory-smoked bacon, soaked
in barbecue sauce (page 49)

1. Tear a ¼-inch-wide strip of husk off each ear of corn to use as a tie. Set aside.

2. Gently peel back the remaining husks on each ear, being careful not to rip them and leaving them attached at the stem end. Pull away as much of the silk as possible, then rub the kernels with a damp towel to remove any remaining silk.

3. Wrap 2 strips of bacon around each ear of corn, then carefully pull the husks back up over the corn and tie at the top with the reserved cornhusk strips. Wrap the prepared ears in a heavy white terry cloth towel, place the towel in the sink, and fill the sink with cold water. Allow to sit for 25 to 30 minutes.

4. Remove the ears from the towel and place on a grill over a medium-hot fire. Cook for about 20 minutes, turning often. Shuck and eat at once.

Company Linen

Every once in a while, kin from Up North would arrive before we got their letter telling us they were coming for a visit (we didn't have a telephone). Naturally, they would be planning to stay at our house and would expect everything to be ready for them. So my mother always had trunks prepared with everything she would need in case of unexpected guests. In one trunk were table linens, in another the good bed linens, including the embroidered pillowcases. Like my grandfather's mama, Aunt Vestula was a fine needlewoman, and her pillowcases with tatting and little flowers made of colored thread had been passed down to my mother. The trunk with these bed linens was kept in the company room. It didn't have a cedar lining, but Mama would cut fresh pieces of cedar and wrap them in brown paper and put them in the trunk. Oh, the smell of fresh cedar that came out of that trunk when it was opened. I still have the trunk, but the pillowcases and other fancy linens have long since disappeared.

"PICK OF THE DAY" STIR-FRY VEGETABLES

Serves 6 to 8

Most fresh summer vegetables do well in this stir-fry side dish. Just be sure that the oil is really hot before you start cooking, and also be careful not to overcook the vegetables or they will become mushy.

4 small yellow squash, washed
6 small zucchini, washed
4 tablespoons olive oil
4 firm, ripe medium tomatoes, stemmed and roughly chopped
2 cups freshly cut corn kernels (about 4 ears)
2 cups chopped green onions (including green part)
1 teaspoon minced garlic
1 teaspoon minced jalapeño pepper
2 teaspoons chopped fresh parsley
1 teaspoon chopped fresh sage
Salt and freshly ground black pepper to taste
2 tablespoons chopped fresh basil

1. Trim the ends from the yellow squash and zucchini and cut them into slices about ¼ inch thick.

2. In a large skillet, heat the oil over high heat until hot but not smoking. Add the yellow squash and zucchini slices and cook, stirring frequently, for 4 minutes. Add the tomatoes, corn, green onions, garlic, and jalapeño peppers and cook, stirring frequently, for an additional 2 minutes.

3. Add the parsley, sage, and salt and pepper to taste and cook, stirring constantly, for about 6 minutes or until the vegetables are tender but not mushy.

4. Add the basil, stir to mix, and serve at once.

JACK'S EASY BEER BREAD
Makes 1 loaf

This recipe comes from my brother Jarvis, whom we call Jack, and it's the only thing I've ever known him to cook.

3 cups self-rising flour
3 tablespoons sugar
One 12-ounce can beer, room temperature
3 tablespoons butter, melted

1. Preheat oven to 350° F. Grease and flour a 9" x 5" x 3" loaf pan.

2. In a large bowl, combine the flour and sugar and mix well. Pour in the beer gradually, stirring constantly, just until the mixture is fully moistened; you may not need the entire can.

3. Spoon the mixture into the prepared pan and bake in the preheated oven for 55 to 60 minutes or until the top is nicely browned, brushing the top with the melted butter after the first 30 minutes.

4. Cool the loaf in the pan for 10 minutes on a wire rack. Remove from the pan and cool completely on the rack before serving.

NEIGHBOR CAKE
Serves 8 to 10

Wonderful recipes are created when a cook finds out only an hour or so before supper that there will be one more mouth to feed. One of my favorites is this cake, which gets its name from the fact that any ingredients you don't have in the house can be easily borrowed. From one neighbor borrow a cup of butter, from another two cups of sugar or three cups of flour, from another four eggs. Pretty soon you'll be ready to make your cake.

This simple cake is best eaten warm, when its delicate flavor is strongest.

2 cups sugar
1 cup butter, softened
3 cups all-purpose flour
½ teaspoon salt
1 tablespoon baking powder
1 cup milk
1 teaspoon vanilla extract
1 teaspoon lemon extract
4 large eggs, lightly beaten

1. Preheat oven to 350° F. Grease and flour a 9-inch tube pan.

2. In a large bowl, cream together the sugar and butter, beating until light and fluffy. In a second bowl, sift together the flour, salt, and baking powder. In a third bowl, combine the milk, extracts, and eggs and beat lightly. Add the wet and dry mixtures to the creamed sugar and butter alternately in three parts, beating after each addition until well mixed.

3. Spoon the batter into the greased and floured pan and bake in the preheated oven for 55 to 60 minutes or until the top is golden and a knife inserted in the cake comes out clean. Cool on a wire rack for 8 minutes, then carefully remove from the pan. Serve warm, or cool completely on the rack.

Curing Sweet Potatoes

Besides peaches, on our farm we always grew many other fruits and vegetables. When I was young, we even grew cotton. My siblings and I were such poor cotton pickers, though, that my daddy abandoned cotton and started growing sweet potatoes in its place. Of course, the dreaded boll weevil probably played a major role in his decision as well. Whatever the reason, I know that when I was a child, we began to harvest thousands of bushels of sweet potatoes every year.

During the fall sweet potato harvest, which used to take place during the first two weeks in October, we had lots of hired help. Besides grown-ups, students from the nearby high schools also came to work in our fields. The experienced workers were sent first to gather the potatoes from the freshly plowed-up rows, because they knew how to select only Grade A potatoes. These potatoes were to be sold, so they were handled carefully with cotton-gloved hands and placed gently in baskets. The potatoes left in the fields for the less experienced pickers didn't have to be handled so gently.

Sweet potatoes will not last the winter unless they are cured. Curing also makes a sweet potato taste better. I believe this is because the white sap found in freshly harvested sweet potatoes is binding and makes the potato dry and chewy, and curing somehow gets rid of the sap, making the potato juicy. We had two special buildings on the farm used only for curing the crop. They were called sweet potato houses, and they were located between the barns and our house.

As the potatoes were harvested, they were brought to the sweet potato houses, wood frame buildings with heavy, hinged cedar doors about eight inches thick. The doors had been specially designed and made by my daddy.

The floors inside the sweet potato houses were hard-packed dirt. Along each wall were slatted bins, each big enough to hold eight to ten bushels of sweet potatoes. Long, fairly narrow strips of lumber like the wood strips used as supports for a bed mattress formed the floors of these bins. The slatted-wood construction allowed for even heat circulation and ventilation. In the center of each sweet potato house was a big potbellied wood-burning iron stove that supplied the heat for curing.

The curing process did not begin until the houses were filled with potatoes. Here's where having sons came in handy. My brothers and father worked well into the nights during the harvest, emptying the heavy bushels of potatoes carefully into the bins to avoid bruising.

When the bins were full of potatoes, the big stove in each sweet potato house was fired up. You could use coal to start the fire, but after the fire got going you didn't want to use coal anymore, because the fumes would affect the taste of the potatoes. So for the rest of the curing we used only oak wood that had been cut to the proper size and stored until the sweet potatoes were ready.

Once the fire in a house was well stoked, the giant cedar doors were closed tightly. For the next week or so, they would be opened only to check the temperature and to maintain the fire. We kept a close watch on the temperature. If it got too high, we opened the doors; if it went too low, we built up the fire some more. You had to hold the temperature just right twenty-four hours a day for eight to ten days.

I don't know if the sweet potatoes you find in the stores today are cured with heat. I do know that *we* don't cure them that way anymore, since we no longer harvest a large acreage of sweet potatoes. Most of the few hundred bushels we now harvest are sold during the late summer and early fall at the farm stand. We store the rest for our own use during the winter in dry, well-ventilated places where the temperature is constant, around fifty to sixty degrees. Where are those places? The crawl spaces in the basements of the homes of my sister Virginia and my brother Orestus. Storing sweet potatoes in this manner is a form of curing, too, but I must admit that the potatoes do not get that wonderfully sweet, intense flavor they have when heat is used for curing.

Sweet potatoes were always a favorite in our family. We used them in salads, casseroles, breads, cakes—just about any way you can imagine. I still love their wonderful taste, and whenever I cook with them, I recall those childhood days of planting and harvesting and the sweet smell of the oak-wood smoke coming from the sweet potato houses.

THE RECIPES

Sweet Potato Soup
Sweet Potato–Raisin Salad
Chilled Sweet Potato Salad with Sweet Pickles and Onions
Sweet Potato Pancakes
Sweet Potato Pound Cake with Peach Glaze

SWEET POTATO SOUP
Serves 4 to 6

This tasty soup, rich in flavor, can be served either hot or cold. If you don't have enough sweet potatoes on hand, you can partially or completely substitute white potatoes.

½ cup butter
1 cup chopped onion
3 cups sweet potato, peeled and cubed
(about 3 large or 5 small potatoes)
1 teaspoon salt, or to taste
3 cups chicken stock (you can substitute 3 cups water
plus 3 chicken bouillon cubes)
2 cups milk
1 teaspoon freshly ground black pepper, or to taste
1 tablespoon minced fresh chives
½ teaspoon paprika

1. In a deep saucepan, melt ¼ cup of the butter over medium-high heat. Add the onions and saute, stirring occasionally, until they are translucent, about 5 minutes.

2. Add the sweet potatoes, salt, and chicken stock, bring to a boil, reduce heat to low, and cover. Simmer for about 40 minutes or until the sweet potatoes are very tender. (For smoother soup, puree in a blender or food processor).

3. Add the remaining ¼ cup butter, the milk, and the pepper. Stir gently to mix and continue to heat, stirring occasionally, until the butter has melted. If you wish to serve the soup cold, remove from heat and allow to cool to room temperature. If you are going to serve it hot, continue to warm over low heat, being careful not to bring to a boil. Serve with chives and paprika sprinkled on top.

SWEET POTATO-RAISIN SALAD
Serves 6 to 8

One day I had to leave the farm stand in the middle of the afternoon to cook supper for some relatives who had come for an unexpected visit. When one of my customers heard about this, she went home with the fresh sweet potatoes she had just bought, made this sweet potato–raisin salad from a recipe I'd posted on the recipe swap board, and hand-delivered the salad to my house.

**3 cups sweet potato, peeled and freshly grated
(about 3 large or 5 small potatoes)
1 cup firm apple, peeled and chopped
1 tablespoon fresh lemon juice (you can substitute pineapple juice)
½ cup dark seedless raisins
⅛ teaspoon each: ground cinnamon, ground nutmeg
½ cup mayonnaise
Loose lettuce leaves, rinsed and dried**

1. In a medium bowl, combine the sweet potato, apple, lemon juice, raisins, cinnamon, and nutmeg and toss lightly.

2. Add the mayonnaise and stir to combine. Cover and refrigerate for 1 to 4 hours.

3. Line a medium glass bowl with the lettuce leaves, mound the salad on top of the leaves, and serve.

CHILLED SWEET POTATO SALAD WITH SWEET PICKLES AND ONIONS

Serves 4 to 6

There is no better dish for a picnic or cookout than this salad. Vidalia onions are best for this recipe, but any sweet onion will do.

4 cups cubed sweet potato (about 4 large potatoes)
1 cup sour cream
2 tablespoons chopped fresh parsley
1 tablespoon fresh lemon juice
1 teaspoon sugar
½ teaspoon celery seed
⅛ teaspoon dill
¼ teaspoon paprika
¼ teaspoon ground white pepper, or to taste
½ teaspoon salt, or to taste
½ cup chopped celery
½ cup chopped sweet pickles
⅔ cup chopped sweet onion (Vidalia, Bermuda, Spanish red, or other variety)
Crisp salad greens, rinsed and dried

1. In a large pot of boiling water, cook the cubed sweet potatoes until they are tender but still offer some resistance when pierced with a fork, about 8 to 10 minutes. Set aside to cool.

2. In a small bowl, combine the sour cream, parsley, lemon juice, sugar, celery seed, dill, paprika, pepper, and salt and mix to combine. Set aside. In a large bowl, combine the cooled sweet potatoes, celery, pickles, and onion.

3. Add all but 2 tablespoons of the sour cream dressing to the potato mixture and mix well. Cover and refrigerate overnight or at least until thoroughly chilled.

4. Turn chilled salad out onto a bed of greens, spoon the reserved dressing over the top, and serve.

Iron Washing Pots

The giant cast-iron pots in our canning house were meant for cooking foods to be canned and for cooking the sweet potatoes we fed to the two hogs we fattened every year. Two other large black cast-iron pots mounted on bricks outside the canning house were used for washing clothes. But on wash days when it was really cold and rainy, my mama would use one of the pots in the canning house to boil clothes. I loved the warmth, the smell of freshly spread sawdust, the sweet potatoes cooking in the other pot, and the peanuts roasting in the hot ashes. It didn't matter what the weather was outside, I was warm and happy in the canning house.

SWEET POTATO PANCAKES
Makes about 1 dozen

I use the sweet, juicy sweet potatoes from our farm to make many of the dishes I remember from my childhood. This one, simple and delicious, is a wonderful side dish for any meal, but it's particularly good topped with freshly made molasses for breakfast.

3 medium sweet potatoes (about 2 pounds)
1 teaspoon fresh lemon juice
2 eggs, lightly beaten
¼ cup grated onion (about ½ medium onion)
2 tablespoons all-purpose flour
¾ teaspoon salt
A dash of nutmeg
A dash of freshly ground black pepper
About 3 tablespoons vegetable oil

1. Wash and peel the sweet potatoes, grate coarsely, sprinkle with the lemon juice, and set aside.

2. In a large bowl, beat the eggs lightly. Add the grated onion, flour, salt, nutmeg, and pepper and mix well. Add the potatoes and mix well again.

3. Pour the oil into a heavy skillet and heat over medium-high heat until hot but not smoking. Drop the batter into the oil by heaping table-spoons, flattening each dollop against the bottom of the pan. Do not crowd the skillet. Fry until golden-brown and crisp, about 3 minutes

per side. Drain well on paper towels and serve hot, topped with fresh molasses and butter.

SWEET POTATO POUND CAKE WITH PEACH GLAZE
Serves 6 to 8

This moist, tasty variation on pound cake is similar to carrot cake but a bit lighter in texture, so if you don't have any sweet potatoes on hand you can substitute carrots—but you won't get that wonderful, rich sweet potato flavor.

1 cup unsalted butter, softened
2 cups sugar
2 ½ cups cooked and mashed sweet potatoes
(about 2 ½ large or 4 small potatoes)
4 eggs
3 cups all-purpose flour
1 teaspoon salt
2 teaspoons baking powder
1 teaspoon baking soda
½ teaspoon ground nutmeg
1 teaspoon ground cinnamon
1 teaspoon vanilla extract

For the glaze:

**⅓ cup drained canned peaches or cooked fresh peaches
(about 1 medium peach)
1 cup confectioners' sugar
½ teaspoon vanilla extract
2 tablespoons milk**

1. Preheat oven to 350° F.

2. In a large bowl, cream the butter and sugar, beating until light and fluffy. Add the sweet potatoes and again beat until light and fluffy. Add the eggs one at a time, beating well after each addition.

3. In a medium bowl, combine the flour, salt, baking powder, baking soda, nutmeg, and cinnamon and stir well. Add to the creamed mixture in three parts, beating after each addition until well combined. Add the vanilla and beat until well combined.

4. Spoon the batter into a large greased and floured tube pan, smooth the top, and bake in the preheated oven for 1 hour and 15 minutes or until the top is just golden-brown and a knife inserted into the cake comes out clean. Remove from oven and cool on a wire rack for 3 minutes, then remove from the pan and cool completely on the rack.

5. While the cake is cooling, mash the canned or cooked fresh peaches to form a puree. Combine in a small bowl with all the remaining glaze ingredients and mix well. Drizzle over the top of the cooled cake.

Kitchen and Herb Gardens

The garden soil is ready. I draw a sketch of the little piece of ground where I will plant my kitchen and herb gardens. I buy onion sets, cabbage and tomato plants, and some herb plants from our local greenhouse. My herb and vegetable seeds, ordered in late winter, are on hand, ready for planting. Every year I yield to the temptation to try something new. This year it will be radicchio.

Both gardens are small enough to be worked by hand. To prepare the soil, I use a fork spade instead of a shovel, and I break the dirt clods as I dig. The soil was also turned in the fall and manure was added then. Now a spring soil test sample will show how much lime is needed. My rake serves as a light cultivator, then I turn to the hoe to build a bed or a row for planting. Before long, my gardens will be planted and I will start looking forward to the first harvest.

These gardens require hardly any space. Let me assure you, a little plot no more than eight by ten feet is plenty of room to plant your own fruits, vegetables, and herbs. Don't plant too many, though, because there's no way to stagger your harvest! And remember, it's hard to raise corn in a small space. But don't worry, I will plant some for you.

INDEX